ACCOUNT RENDERED

Sir Ernest Benn has also written

THE CONFESSIONS OF A CAPITALIST

IF I WERE A LABOUR LEADER

THE LETTERS OF AN INDIVIDUALIST

TRADE

THE CASE OF BENN *v.* MAXTON
(*with Mr. James Maxton, M.P.*)

PRODUCER *v.* CONSUMER

THE RETURN TO LAISSER FAIRE

ABOUT RUSSIA

UNEMPLOYMENT AND WORK

ACCOUNT RENDERED

1900–1930

*being an attempt to estimate the moral and
material cost of the new ideas expressed
in the political activities of Great
Britain during this period*

by

ERNEST J. P. BENN

LONDON 1930
ERNEST BENN LIMITED

First Published in
1930
Printed
in
Great Britain

FOREWORD

If the figures in this book require some correction and if parts of the argument are open to question, the general conclusion remains, I think, true. It is that by our political folly we have put a large part, probably the greater part, of the nation in possession of rights to draw from the public purse. Whether those rights take the form of relief, dole, pension, official salary, subsidy or interest on public debt, they all constitute heavy claims on our total production. If happily, we manage to escape national bankruptcy, we have set up a slavery for the minority, the producers, far more oppressive than any previous form of bondage—all because we alone among the nations of Europe persist in thinking ourselves better off than before the war, have forgotten the meaning of economy and settled down to the enjoyment of the "fruits of victory." We are interested in our wages rather than our work, in the price rather than the product, are obsessed with the spirit of grab and decline to give value for value.

"... And they shall teach no more every man his neighbour, and every man his brother ..."

JEREMIAH xxxi. 34.

" Let's stop somebody from doing some-
    thing !
    Everybody does too much.
People seem to think they've a right to
    eat and drink,
Talk and walk and respirate and rink,
    Bicycle and bathe and such.
So let's have lots of little regulations,
Let's make laws and jobs for our
    relations,
There's too much kissing at the railway
    stations—
Let's find out what everyone is doing,
    And then stop everyone from doing it."

A. P. HERBERT.

CONTENTS

CHAPTER I

THE PURPOSE OF THE ACCOUNT

AFTER thirty years of the new politics there may be some wisdom in an endeavour to make up the account. Indeed, something in the nature of a statement of our position is forced upon us by the processes familiar to all who possess a purse or a banking account. There comes a time when even the most careful of us finds that the balance is low, the ability to draw a cheque is limited, and when we cannot escape the unpleasant exercise of setting out the figures on the one side and the other so that we may know the amount of the balance, and whether it may be called a credit or a debit. Wise people do this sort of thing weekly or quarterly or yearly; the spendthrifts do it only when they are forced. Some folk are incapable of doing it, and the task has to be performed for them by liquidators or receivers in bankruptcy. But however it may be performed, the individual or the nation is always liable to the risk of facing the account. The necessity is less obvious with the nation than with the individual, and nations do not, therefore, always exercise the caution and care which the individual ordinarily gives to his financial affairs. The individual always knows that he is spending his own money, while the nation is apt to think of the matter less directly. It is free, or appears to be free, from the inconvenient arrival of the creditor in the shape of a summons or a broker's man. It gets into financial difficulties, and then, in the exercise of what it is pleased to call its sovereign rights, repudiates its debts, inflates its currency, or, as in our own case, pretends to find commercial credit in future generations; calls it "gilt-edged" (a gilt which in this connection ought really to be spelt with a "u"), and somehow gets away with it. There is, it need hardly be said, no real difference in this respect between the humblest individual and the proudest nation. Both are under the obligation to pay their way and both face the risk of bankruptcy, that risk being more serious in the case of the nation, because of the greater difficulty of making exact accounts and of obtaining an accurate statement of the position at any particular moment.

It is open to question whether the methods hitherto used for national accountancy are still adequate in view of the new habits of the new politics whereby ever larger future commitments are continuously created. Individual accounts have always had some consideration for the future; a responsible person does not take a seven-year lease of a house, or enter his children for an expensive and long educational course, unless he has a very reasonable expectation that the rent or the expenses will be available out of his own visible resources. But a nation sells a Savings Certificate, or guarantees a sixty-year loan to some subsidiary enterprise, without any such restraints or precautions. It rests content in the knowledge that comparatively small public debts have always, in the past, found someone to honour them, and it presumes, upon this experience, that the future is good for any amount, however fantastic, to which it cares to set the seal of its authority. The national Budget has hitherto been no more than a statement of cash received and paid during the year, and there were good and weighty reasons for this course when Budgets dealt with reasonable figures and when the nation had the habit of more or less paying its way. Now, however, when week by week Parliament piles more and more responsibility upon the future, there is an obvious need for a second Budget which shall tell us, in addition to our cash position, the truth about our liabilities.

Our case is very different from that of the Austrians or the Germans, the Russians, or even the French, for we not only hold a unique position as the trustees for the world of security and stability, but we actually live on that position. If our accounts ceased to attract the respect of the world, we should starve. There can therefore be no question of our unanimous determination to maintain our position as the authors and guardians of economic rectitude, and, that being so, the time has arrived when we ought to pause, take stock, make up a profit and loss account and a balance sheet, and generally render to ourselves a statement of our doings and see where we stand.

We have just completed thirty years of the new politics. All those progressive ideas which were incubating in the late eighties and throughout the nineties may be said to have hatched out with the arrival of Mr. Lloyd George about the year 1900, to have become fully fledged in the "People's Budget" of 1909, and to have dominated our thoughts and actions ever since. We have arranged our taxes according to ability to pay. We have distributed our benefits as measured by the apparent needs. We have invented and glorified the notion of public credit. Money has been spent like water on all sorts of public purposes. The State, represented by Imperial Parliament or by the parish council, has accepted responsibilities and liabilities never thought or heard of before the era of the new politics. Dreams that were scouted as wild and fantastic when they first came from the offices of the Fabian Society have since formed the basis of Conservative programmes, and the whole nation has thrown itself into the greatest concerted effort of all time to rectify through the use of political force the supposed evils arising from the workings of economic law. More than thirty years have passed since Sir William Harcourt said with prophetic truth that "we are all Socialists now," and in that thirty years our public liabilities have multiplied not less than thirty times.

One big item in the Account Rendered which we propose to consider must be mentioned only for the sake of accuracy and in order that it may be dismissed. Whenever I meet a man in trouble, whenever I come across any little personal difficulty in my own circle, the chances are that the war will be used as an excuse for evils caused by

some other folly. The war left us with a debt of
£7,000,000,000 – ten times the pre-war figure.
It involved us in an annual charge of £350,000,000,
and is an item which can be put into an account by
itself, and provided for as one – almost the only
one – of our liabilities capable of exact measurement and precise definition. When, however, we
come to realise, as we must do sooner or later, that
the amount of the bill which we have to hand on to
posterity, as a direct result of our post-war actions
alone, is far heavier than the cost of the whole of
the war itself, we shall get 1914–18, with all its
horrors, into a better financial and economic
perspective.

It must be said to the credit of our politicians
that in this year 1930 they are talking rather less
about the war. When they call attention to some
great evil, with the obvious deduction that we
should vote for some particular party in order to
remove it, they do not now quote the war with the
frequency, regularity, or emphasis which was
common a few years ago. The fashion in politics
has changed, and we hear now about "world
conditions." When the legislative efforts of 1928
or 1929 prove in 1930 to be mere stupidities,
statesmen make speeches and plead that world
conditions are against them. Thus in making up
our Account Rendered it is well for us to know that
some allowances require to be made on account of
happenings in other parts of the globe. It is, for
instance, obvious that when our rulers in their
wisdom arranged for Germany to export coal free of

all charge the position of our own coal exporters
became extremely difficult. We are, however, in-
dulging in a self-deceit unworthy of an educated
people if we imagine that more than a small
fraction of such troubles as face us is due to any
causes other than those which can be found at
home. Without attempting to minimise the importance of our overseas business, both import
and export, our arithmetical sense should be
sufficient to remind us that ten or fifteen per cent.,
at the most, is the measure of this part of our
economic affairs. Most of our business is done with
one another at home. Most of our opportunities
arise from the needs of our neighbours. Most of
our development, if we are capable of further
development, is to be made in the many more ways
in which we can be of service one to another within
the confines of our own island. Home trade can be
expanded almost without limit if we want to work,
if we desire to serve others, or if we desire to raise
the standard of living, and our overseas business,
important as it is, amounts to no more than a
useful and necessary section of our activities. We
export and import for the very simple reason that
we must eat. When Mill and Cobden wrote and
spoke, the feeding of our people was a very difficult
matter. To-day, with the development of education
and what is called civilisation, feeding has ceased
to be the biggest of man's problems, and we live
for other and better things. All of which is not to
say that food is not vital and that our overseas
trade need not be maintained, but merely to point

out that 85 to 90 per cent. of our activities are now concerned with other matters.

The period of the new politics, which has brought us up against the necessity of reckoning the cost and making up an account, has been characterised in a very human and natural way by a highly vocal disdain of everything that happened before this wonderful era of progress began. No social stigma was ever more deadly than the suspicion attached to anyone in public affairs of entertaining any sympathy with Victorian manners or methods. This very marked tendency, this very definite change of view, makes our task a little easier. Had the change in our thoughts and ways been less violent, it might be much more difficult to draw useful comparisons and to get an account on which definite conclusions could be based, but the complete denial of Victorian philosophy and Victorian political economy gives us a clear-cut comparison that will be of value to us, for accountancy is a useless waste of time and effort except as a means of comparison. Figures in themselves mean nothing, unless they indicate alteration, difference, increase, or decrease. When a shareholder receives the annual account of a company in which he is interested, the amount of the capital or the cash or the stock or the liabilities matters very little to him. What he seeks to know is how these items stand in relation to previous figures. If liabilities have increased, he looks for a corresponding, or hopes for a greater, increase in assets. If assets have diminished, he expects to see that certain liabilities have

also disappeared. The actual figure of the balance
on the account brings neither grief nor joy to him,
but he attaches great importance to the fact that
the balance is more or less than was previously
shown. Accountancy is a comparative science.
Before proceeding, therefore, to write up the
accounts for the new political era, it will be convenient and, indeed, necessary to glance at the
previous balance sheet so that we may know in
what respects the position has improved, and in
what ways it is worse.

We cannot be good judges of the economic situation unless we know the condition of the national
estate in the time of our grandfathers and our
fathers, and also unless we have in our minds a clear
conception of the position in which we would like
our sucessors to stand. Economics is not worthy of
study if it is concerned with no more than our own
immediate needs and desires.

CHAPTER II

THE VICTORIANS

THE nineteenth century possessed many characteristics which have happily passed into history, and we in the twentieth enjoy a good deal of freedom from intellectual and social conventions upheld and suffered by our grandfathers. It may be because of some divine limitation which operates to keep this world still merely human, but, even so, it seems a pity that while discarding the social failings of our grandfathers we have also found it necessary to throw away most of their economic wisdom.

The nineteenth century witnessed economic development on a scale never before or since approached. The study of progress shows that it is a long process, sometimes hastened and sometimes retarded according to the point of view of succeeding generations. Solid progress has been made whenever a generation has been willing to pay due respect to the past, to profit from its legacies, to build upon them, and to leave to the future something more than it inherited. The nineteenth century conformed to all these requirements. Every generation left something over for the next. The Victorians were always working to build up the capital account, as distinguished from our weakness for living on credit. They were denied the advantage, or the curse – for there are two points of view in the matter – of a highly developed

financial machine which makes it very easy for us
to juggle with capital. Their politicians were limited
to the £70,000,000 or £80,000,000 or £90,000,000
which was the total that they ever put into a
national Budget. They had their inflation in the
Napoleonic wars, but it was only a trifle compared
with the way in which we manufactured money
in the Great War of 1914–18. The Victorians were
thinking of bricks and mortar, while we are concerned with book-keeping credits. They paid cash
for their bricks and mortar, and left the tangible
article to render service to the future. We put up
breeze-block boxes to look like houses, do not pay
cash, but pass on inflated bills which will mature
in the future when the flimsy structures have
disappeared.

The building up of national security and prosperity differs in no way from the building up of a
family position or the steady development of a
business enterprise. In the case of the family, there
are not many fathers who do not endeavour to
some extent to save up something for the benefit of
their children. The ambition of every good parent
is to put the child in a rather better social and
economic position than the father. The idea behind
that common family ambition, if allowed to operate
freely, builds up a similar improving national
position. The ambition in the case of the family
does not always succeed. It will sometimes override
itself, and, by taking too much risk, a family will
come to grief; but the nation is safe provided that
all the families are doing something of this kind and

that the majority of them achieve a measure of success. These problems, so simple when approached from a family point of view, are no less simple when they concern a nation. The best of families will produce every so often a weak or unworthy or unfortunate generation, and then the degrading spectacle is witnessed of lives of idleness or pleasure spent out of capital, ending with mortgages, foreclosures, and penury. Then the family starts again. That sort of thing is sad enough in the case of a single family, but when a nation adopts the same habits we witness a check to progress involving all the families of the future in a lower standard of living.

If the nation be regarded as a business firm, and the principles which are recognised as good for business be applied to national affairs, then almost everything which has been done in the last thirty years is, on the face of it, bad. No business that has any claim to be considered as a serious undertaking ever distributed or spent the whole of its product. An essential feature of any commercial balance sheet is the amount which is placed to reserve or carried forward to the future. In the nineteenth century, before the days of limited liability companies and without very much in the way of banking accommodation, the reserves made by business men were, perforce, represented by genuine values. Bit by bit new buildings or new stocks or new machines were accumulated, and year by year the capital account became of more value. The tendency to-day, forced upon the business community by the nature of our taxation, is to capitalise future income instead of past surpluses. As soon as we think we can see an earning capacity of a few thousands a year, we rush to the City, sell it for fifteen or twenty years' purchase, create a capital which is represented by nothing but future earning power, and proceed to live upon the proceeds. The result is that whereas the inheritors of a nineteenth-century business found themselves possessed of mills and machines and stocks of raw materials, the unfortunate inheritors of a modern company often find nothing but a big nominal capital account on which by hook or by crook they must find a way of paying a dividend. From whatever point of view we approach the matter, it seems clear that in these enlightened times we are able to find ways of living on our capital, whereas in the nineteenth century a large part of the national and commercial effort was directed to an endeavour to improve the position of the future. This distinction is the more striking because the nineteenth century is not associated in our minds with any particular desire to care for its children, whereas we of the twentieth century never cease boasting of our determination to look after the young people. It cannot, however, be long before we discover that in economics the important thing is what we do and not what we think. Motives have their uses in their proper place, but in the economic and material world motives do not serve as securities for overdrafts.

The nineteenth century, while making most of

the wealth that brings us comfort to-day, did not appear to be conscious of a desire to provide for our happiness. Its children were brought up in the fear of the bogeyman. They were the poor little victims of a system of education and training which we think barbarous and wrong. They were put into factories and coal-mines. Only the fittest of them could survive. Lady Wood, the mother of Mrs. Parnell and a lady of the Bedchamber to Queen Caroline, had thirteen children, and was very proud of the fact that seven of them survived. So that it is absurd to pretend that the economic wisdom of the nineteenth century arose out of a conscious desire to make things better for future generations. But they did, from whatever incentive, possess or acquire a knowledge which seems to have entirely forsaken us. They knew that civilised life, from its very nature, is, and must always be, a struggle with the forces of nature. They entertained no foolish illusions about the possibility of organising comfort and happiness. Indeed, comfort and happiness, in their more manly philosophy, were not altogether respectable things. We have altered all that. We have reversed every theory upon which these people founded their position as the acknowledged leaders of the civilised world, and in particular we have made it our business to see that the child from his birth has every comfort lavished upon him and every personal responsibility removed from him. It is permissible to wonder whether this child, so equipped, will be anything like strong enough to shoulder economic burdens which the child of the nineteenth century never knew.

As we walk or drive about this little island of ours, nine-tenths of everything we see and use and enjoy was put there by our Victorian forefathers. They built our towns, including those parts now regarded as slums. They built our factories and our mansions. They laid our drains, put down our railways, equipped us with our water and our gas. And they paid for them. In addition, year by year they spread our properties right over the map, built nine-tenths of the railways of the world, and left them for us to inherit. Few of us pause to remember that three-quarters of all the houses that we see on the land were actually built between 1850 and 1900, and not only built, but paid for. There were very wonderful building societies even in those days, but their figures would be considered insignificant by any modern borough council, however small. These building societies lent money on mortgage, never more than two-thirds of a hard cash value, and their total debt represented but a very small fraction of the price of the houses built in this period. We have done, since the war, a little bit of building. Notice, however, the striking difference between the Victorian house and ours. Examples can be found in every parish. Almost side by side one can see a solid brick villa built for £250, with a building society loan of £160 spread over fifteen years and long since paid, and an Addison or a Wheatley house which cost £1,000, which will be in ruins long before its Victorian counterpart, and on which a 90 per cent. loan is standing in the books of the local authority. The house is costing the present ratepayers £1 a week in interest alone, the tenant is paying 10s. a week in rent, no provision of any kind is made for depreciation or replacement, the £1,000 of nominal value has already shrunk to £500 and will sooner or later have depreciated to £200. The contrast, considered in the light of the obligations of one generation to another, is indeed a striking one. The hard, practical methods of the Victorians applied uniformly to family, to business, and to State affairs put us at the very head of civilisation, for in the eighties there was no nation, not even the United States of America, which could approach us in any economic test. Trade or wealth per head of population, use of steam power, consumption of commodities – test us how you will, we topped the list on every score. All doubt on this question is set aside by Sir Robert Giffen in his presidential address to the Royal Statistical Society in 1883.[1]

The infant born in Great Britain about that time was the most favoured of all creatures in a world which set small value upon infant life or comfort. He inherited the hard work of a century, and with it he inherited a debt of not more than £18, for the total national and local liabilities in 1900 amounted to £18 per head of the population. Things have changed very considerably since those days, and the infant who has the luck to be born

[1] *Economic Inquiries and Studies* : Giffen.

an Englishman in 1930 enters upon life as the
most heavily handicapped of all the infants of the
world. He has to shoulder a liability which is
certainly not less than £500, for in the meantime,
in the name of social service and largely because
of our supposed interest in the child and his
development, we have put upon his tender shoulders national and local debts amounting to at
least £500 per head of the population. We have,
of course, also added something to our assets – a
few houses, though disgracefully few, and not sufficient to keep up with the increase in the population and the wear and tear of existing premises,
and a few roads. Such credit as we may take for
these additions to the public amenities is heavily
discounted by the inflated price at which they will
have to be reckoned in the Account Rendered.

The Victorians are thought by us to have been
materialists, a bad character made worse by their
supposed failure to appreciate the possibilities of
their children. We flatter ourselves into idealists,
and we give a large part of our thoughts to the
perfection of child life. When, however, the
account is rendered and shows that our way of
doing things is heaping liabilities upon posterity,
that each of our children will be burdened with
twenty-five times the amount of debt which we
inherited, then public opinion about these matters
will very rapidly change.

Political economy was known to the Victorians
as the dry-as-dust science, its basic truths were
tacitly accepted and applied, while its technical

discussion was left to such scholars as cared to find their interest that way. The new economics – a horrid word, with no vestige of economy about it – is to us post-war people a joyous game of spending rates and taxes and amassing public debt. These two different and opposite subjects occupy the same place in a University syllabus, but the connection between them is about as strong as the similarity between the old religious service and the modern cinema show which have both made use of the same church building in, say, Moscow.

CHAPTER III

THE POST-WAR MAN

IF the gentle reader be a man or a woman whose experience of the practical things of life is limited to the last fifteen or sixteen years, a further complication is added to the account on which we are engaged. Such a person is thinking in terms and dealing with values very different from those which form the basis of the thought and action of the man whose experience was gained before the war. We have been discussing the Victorians, people whose accounts may be said to have closed with the end of the nineteenth century. We are now dealing with post-war people who have nothing but history to help them with the nineteenth century, and for the most part little but childish recollections of the years 1900 to 1914. The people who were coming to maturity in 1914, and had some personal experience of that transition period, were to a large extent wiped out between 1914 and 1918. Thus the situation has an element of novelty about it, in that we have the small remnants of the Victorians clashing with the greater numbers of the post-war generation, and are robbed of the connecting link between them – the 1900–14 generation.

Those years were spent in developing the social and political policy which has since completely overwhelmed us. The people who conducted our affairs from the beginning of the century to the outbreak of war had the advantage of an intimate knowledge of the past with which to temper and adjust the novelty of new ideas. But we of to-day are faced with still more new ideas, and the necessity of trying them out and finding the good or the bad that is in them, without that advantage – on the whole a very difficult and risky task. So, before setting out the details of the account which it is our purpose to render, there may be some wisdom in an endeavour to indicate a few of the most striking differences in social and economic outlook between the post-war citizen and his Victorian predecessor.

The first typical illustration that occurs to me is this question of wages and the cost of living, a completely new and, as it seems to some of us, false idea which has settled down upon society, which was never thought of in Victorian times and little heard of until the war. At least a thousand millions of war debt and about a quarter of our costs and debts since 1918 are directly due to the new idea that the worker or producer can justify his price, not by the value given, but by his needs or costs. The Victorian believed that the buyer settled the price. He understood that his wages must come out of the money paid by the buyer. He took the view that the purpose of industry was to deliver the goods, and it never entered his head that there was any other excuse for the existence of an industry. When he built a railway (and, of course, he built all the railways) he started on the principle that the freight rate must be "what the traffic would bear." He recognised that his wages as a railway worker were absolutely limited by the willingness of the community to put money into the booking-office or over the goods counter. It never dawned upon him that he could have any claim except that which could be met from the money in the coffers of the railway company, put there by free and willing passengers who made use of the service which he offered. He was fully and painfully conscious that his work as a porter or a shunter was to provide a railway service for which others would be willing to pay. It never occurred to him that his domestic complications, the number of his children, or other special requirements, had anything to do with the price he should receive for shunting or portering. And he bequeathed to us a railway system which, tested by any standard of utility, was a better social service in 1900 than it is in 1930. The Victorian market in railways and in everything else was firmly grounded upon the theory that if the producers or the merchants kept the convenience of the consumer or the buyer uppermost in their minds, then prosperity for all would follow as surely as night follows day. The Victorian, as a worker or as a business man, never conceived it possible that he might have any rights; he only recognised his responsibilities and his obligation to serve. The cost of living was a reason for his wanting a wage, but it had nothing whatever to do with the way he might get it.

As with wages, so with the selling price of the

finished article. No Victorian business man ever attempted to justify a price by the cost of the article. His skill was directed to the more troublesome task of accommodating the cost to the price. He did not, in post-war fashion, pile up extravagant costs by pandering to the supposed needs and rights of all associated with production, and then try to find a market for an article at a price which few could pay. He adopted exactly the opposite method, first endeavouring to discover what was the price at which a sufficient quantity of his article could be sold, and then applying himself by study and research and work to surmount all the difficulties of producing the article within that figure. Thus we see that the approaches to an industrial or commercial proposition of the Victorian and the post-war man are, in fact, from opposite ends. The Victorians invented the earlier forms of accountancy, and are responsible for the phrase "profit and loss," still used in accounts much as old public house signs hang up long after their meaning is forgotten. It was a recognised part of the business man's task to make losses as well as profits, but the post-war man is living in a world where profits are taboo, from which it follows that losses must be avoided, a statement which to the Victorian would have no meaning. The anti-profit atmosphere in which the new politics thrives apace, makes profits harder to procure and less worth having, damps down enterprise, and multiplies unemployment. The post-war man has been brought up on the principle of "Safety

First." Safety was the last thought that entered
the Victorian's commercial mind. We decline
to work until all inconvenience, danger, and
risk have been eliminated, and the Victorians
would therefore find little reason to wonder that
we are unemployed. There are many people to-day
who would gladly enough vote for an Act of Parliament to abolish loss. Indeed, it is frequently
suggested by persons who do not understand these
matters that losses can be avoided by a process of
insurance, an argument that is likely to carry less
weight when the need for a complete revision of
our ideas about unemployment "insurance" can
no longer be resisted.

The differences between the two schools of
thought can be summed up in a couple of sentences.
The post-war man, from the manufacturer to the
unskilled labourer, says to the world (for nothing
will ever make me believe that he really says it to
himself): "I have a wife and two children, and to
live in the way that I want to live I am faced with
all sorts of expenses. Somebody must therefore put
me on to his pay-roll, or somebody else must be
taxed so that I may have, week by week, a sum of
money which will meet those expenses." Then follows, almost as an incidental detail, some little discussion as to whether this or that class of work is
most suitable or convenient. The Victorian took
another line, and really did say to himself: "I am a
greengrocer [or whatever it might have been]. I
am making £2 a week, and my wife and six children have to screw and pinch to keep themselves

alive. I will therefore try to sell more greengrocery, or I will find some other market in which buyers may be willing to pay me more." That very simple difference in the method of approach sums up the economic difficulties into which we have drifted. The laws of nature were recognised by the Victorian world; we have still to learn that such things exist.

There are many other changes that have come upon the post-war man and woman. The Victorian was actively concerned all through his life with his character. Whether he was forced by circumstances or fired by ambition or spurred on by the spirit of service makes no difference. He aimed all through his life at developing the good opinion of his friends, his neighbours, or his customers, and that good opinion depended upon his personal actions and the quality and quantity of the goods and services which he contributed to the common pool. A business man was peculiarly subject to this pressing necessity for character or reputation. Something of the same kind exists to-day, but the similarity is extremely slight. Personal character is no doubt of value in 1930, but it will avail no man unless his papers are in order. The extension of the system of governmental and other sorts of control has placed upon all of us the necessity of conforming to rules and regulations, of satisfying technical conditions, of acquiring certificates and permits of various kinds which are, in point of fact, of greater importance than personal character. A man may surpass all records in skill as a

carpenter and yet be a bad citizen, an enemy of
society, because he does not possess the appropriate union ticket. A newspaper proprietor may turn
out from week to week the most valuable contributions to literature and to knowledge, and go into
the Bankruptcy Court for the lack of a net sales
certificate duly prepared by auditors and association officials who are ignorant of journalism and do
not know the meaning of knowledge. A merchant
may desire to travel about Europe and spread over
it the advantages of his purchases and his sales, and
will find himself absolutely stopped for the absence
of an indiarubber smudge on a thing called a pass-
port. A large proportion of the thought and effort
of all of us is devoted to the requirements of the
various authorities by whom we are surrounded,
and the question of character never enters into our
dealings with any of them. Card indices, forms and
chits, licences, stamps and tallies, have taken the
place of a tested reputation for right dealing or the
ability to do a job of work well. In the Victorian
days the lower classes of labour had the habit of
collecting "characters." A farm labourer or a
kitchenmaid would produce, when required, a
greasy envelope containing a collection of much-
thumbed letters from clergymen and others, cer-
tifying that their possessor was honest and
sober. The post-war millionaire dare not venture
into the street until he has searched his pockets to
be sure that all his chits and papers are in order.
This sort of difference is most marked in the numerous recent Companies Acts, all drafted upon the

assumption that men can be forced into honesty by files at Somerset House.

The other day there was a newspaper paragraph which was read by post-war readers and Victorians with very different feelings. It illustrates in another way the difference between the two worlds with which we are for the moment concerned. A couple of lodging-house keepers at Southend were prosecuted for touting among visitors at the railway station, and both of them were fined, under some new rule made by the Southend Council in pursuance of the notion that all our acts and doings must be regulated. The post-war woman no doubt says to herself: "How delightful! Here are two of these beastly lodging-house keepers punished for their impertinence and their pushing ways. Why should they be a nuisance to people?" The Victorian looks at the matter through other spectacles. One of the troubles of civilised existence in an over-populated island is that more people desire to go to the seaside at certain seasons than the seaside can accommodate comfortably. The lodging-house keeper is therefore in a position of economic superiority, takes full advantage of it, bleeds her visitors, and is often something of a blot on what might otherwise be a delightful holiday. She has her difficulties, no doubt, with rates and taxes all the year round, and in other ways. But how comforting it is to think that for one season at least the lodging-house keepers of Southend are not the mistresses of the market, are driven to seek for custom, and actually take the trouble to go to the railway station to place their services at the disposal of holiday-makers. In these circumstances the service is likely to be better and the price more reasonable. That is the way in which the Victorian would look at it. He would further notice how the rates and taxes of Southend have been pushed up to the present high figures. The newspaper paragraph tells us that two policemen were specially charged with the duty of preventing these lodging-house women from offering their services at the railway station. Our Victorian probably said to himself: "What a waste of two lives! Here are two policemen, no doubt excellent fellows, each paid two or three times as much as we used to pay a policeman, each with his pension at full rates waiting for him when he has done his twenty-five years' service, and that service takes the absurd, useless, and dangerous form of preventing the lodging-house keeper from plying her trade in a difficult season and delivering summonses to the same woman for the non-payment of rates and taxes when the season is over." There would seem to be nothing but obstruction and uselessness in the lives of these two excellent policemen.

Our post-war people benefit, or suffer – there are two sides to the argument – from all the lavish attention which is given in these days to health and welfare. It never enters their heads that they lose a claim to wages on account of ill-health. Neither do they appear to consider that if that claim is admitted to be good, the cost of it goes into the price which the consumer must pay. They are encouraged from birth to submit to inspection, to invite examination, and to harbour the possibility that there may be something wrong with their tonsils, their appendix, their teeth, or even their mental development. They pass round from clinic to clinic or, if they have the money, from specialist to specialist, and use a great deal of the mental energy which used to be devoted to the convenience of the buyer to a search after trouble within themselves. The West End of London is crowded with specialists making fortunes out of fancied ills. The rest of the town is dotted in every parish with institutions searching about for ills with which to deal. All this comes out of the post-war notion that the individual has no desire to control himself or is incapable of doing so, and that by research, organisation, arrangement, and other forms of forethought, health, happiness, and well-being can be secured for all. No one can doubt that there is a great deal of good in this point of view. No one can deny that the physical standard in some respects is better for all this effort and machinery. It remains to be seen, however, what may be the effect upon the moral character and the intellectual outlook of much of this quite new social habit. The mastery of a mental attitude over one's physical condition is an ethic with a strong appeal to the Victorian school of thought. I am sadly conscious of the fact that morning after morning all through my life I have experienced a disinclination to work. I feel it to be true that, but for the imperative necessity of work, ground into me by my Victorian training, the temptations to avail myself of symptoms which suggested trouble might have been too strong for me. I seem to be up against the doctor and the specialist, the inspector, and all the other persons who would do me good. If one man tells me that some treatment is necessary I go to another, who, for another fee, gives me the opposite opinion, and then I strive to get along with my work in my own way, with a certain moral exhilaration derived from a triumph over what I still regard as soft and dangerous fads. Be that as it may, if it is still true, as I believe it to be, that civilised life is a hard daily struggle with the forces of nature, and that civilisation cannot be maintained without a keen appreciation of the necessity of that struggle deeply rooted in the consciousness of every individual, then the Victorian outlook upon all these things was a healthier and a safer one than that which prevails in the office of the Ministry of Health. I take hope in the thought that most people, even the post-war people, are really of my opinion, and do not accept the ministerial mind at its own valuation.

CHAPTER IV

VALUE FOR MONEY

THE Treasury, the Bank of England, and the money markets of the world have something to do with the processes known as inflation and deflation, but we smaller fry who potter about with our own little jobs as bricklayers or publishers are not without our responsibility even in big movements and highly technical questions like these. A Government may determine upon a policy of inflation and arrange to increase the amount of currency available, but the bricklayers and the publishers, by various subsidiary processes, have it in their power to intensify the evil. It is at this moment far from certain that such effects as have been felt in prices and markets by the monetary actions of our Government are not of less importance than the effects of all the little inflationary processes in which most of us have indulged. If, instead of trying to form opinions upon highly technical questions which he cannot understand, the average elector would examine his own actions, the mass of resulting economic wisdom would put the Treasury and the Bank of England into positions of comparative unimportance.

Money is not an end; it is only a means. The fact that money is scarce or plentiful, is inflated or deflated, will make a good deal of difference to the smooth working of commerce and industry, but it is the solid things – the iron, cloth, paper, or hats – which alone are responsible for a good or bad standard of living. While the Treasury and the Bank of England are obliged to think in terms of money, it is highly desirable for the rest of us to remember that money is nothing but a medium of exchange, and to make our calculations in terms of things. In the actual daily practice of all of us we pay for what we receive with the goods we make or the services we perform. Money is only a convenience to us. The baker pays for everything he wants for himself in loaves of bread, the publisher in books, the railwayman in train miles, and we could avoid much economic folly if only we would form a habit of thinking in terms of the things we do instead of the money we get or pay.

There is a natural price for everything; in fact there are two prices. When a handkerchief is sold for a shilling, the buyer takes the view that the handkerchief is worth more to him than the shilling, and the seller takes the other view and prefers the shilling to the handkerchief. That simple, useful article is therefore worth rather less than a shilling to the seller and rather more than a shilling to the buyer. If it were not so, the handkerchief and the shilling would not be exchanged. The natural price of an article is not a fixed figure, and will vary from time to time and from place to place. Strawberries in London will be worth 6*d*. a lb. in June and 10*s*. a lb. in December. The humble strawberry is one of the few articles that, so far as I know, still submits itself to the natural regulation of the law of supply and demand, although we must expect, if we go farther along the present silly road, to find some chamber of horticulture devising a scheme for limiting the production of strawberries in June, and by a process of rationalisation making the December price uniform throughout the year. That is the sort of thing that has been happening for years past in connection with many of our commodities, and is one of the bad post-war habits to be discarded when economic health returns to us. The natural price of an article, although for convenience we express it as so much money, is really the measure of the effort or sacrifice which others are prepared to make in order to acquire it. Fashion, fancy, opinion, habit, as well as supply and demand, all have something to do with it. The Victorians, for instance, made great sacrifices, gave a large part of their effort, to the acquisition of lace for use on curtains or undergarments, while we, being of another opinion, decline to waste our productive power in the same way. Fashion and fancy have changed. In normal times, and in all places, there is a price which is generally acceptable as fair and proper for any given article or service. This price tends to vary. It will go up or down because of supply or demand, because of the amount of gold coming into the market, because of good or bad harvests, but these things are now less important in their effect compared with a number of quite modern factors which have pushed prices up and down, mostly up, far more drastically.

The new politics, our new game of bossing every action of everybody, and the modern mania for organising everything, exercise far more disturbing effects upon prices than ever occurred by reason of the supply of gold or the state of the harvest.

A series of index numbers of retail prices published in the *Journal of the Royal Statistical Society* of March, 1909, gives us a fair measure of the classical factors which influence price movements.

1850	..	100	1869	..	115	1889	..	91
1854	..	104	1874	..	117	1894	..	90
1859	..	117	1879	..	110	1899	..	85
1864	..	110	1884	..	104	1902	..	90
			1907	..	92			

In half a century, therefore, supply and demand, harvests, gold, and the rest, pushed prices up or down – on the whole, down – but the maximum movement in any period of five years was 13 per cent. The movement was generally slow enough to enable people to accommodate themselves to the new conditions, and until the period of the new politics the world was without experience of schemes which altered prices so violently and so rapidly as to throw millions out of work.

Any action taken by the Treasury in the way of controlling currency has to-day a minor importance to the actions taken by other big Government departments. Currency control may alter the price level a few points, but a State housing scheme can double the price of a house.

A State or a Government going into trade is not subject to the natural restraints and balances that keep the actions of the private individual within the bounds of reason and practicability. The State is paying for what it buys, not in its own efforts, but in the work of other people. As an individual I may decline to give three months of my work to acquire a piano, and, because I have to look at it that way, I am saved from obvious extravagance. But the State wanting an extra piano, because the caretaker in an elementary school does not like the trouble of moving an instrument from one classroom to another, will not hesitate, by taxing me, to sacrifice three months of my work for that purpose. Thus every new activity of a public authority always has an inflationary character and a tendency to extravagance.

Currency experts do not usually talk about education, but when we find that the cost of educating a child in 1913 was £4 per annum, and of educating the same child in 1927 was £16 per annum, and when, on further enquiry, we find that everything that is done in the name of the public has followed a similar course, the fact that the Bank of England has five or six millions more or less of gold bars in its cellars becomes a detail and not a matter of primary importance.

To understand aright the problems involved in national finance we must have a basis of elementary sanity. Somehow or another the majority of the thirty million electors must have a few ideas upon money and prices and values which will stand

Dr

examination. The Victorians were quite sound on
these matters. The Americans to-day are equally
sound, but we have so thoroughly absorbed false
thoughts, like the cost-of-living index figure as a
basis for wage settlements, that our difficulties are
far greater than we ourselves realise. But we shall
waste our time in trying to understand the Account
Rendered unless we will each of us go back to the
beginning and make quite sure that we know what
we mean when we use such words as price or wage
or value. The price of a suit of clothes to me, a
journalist, is not so many sovereigns, although it
has to be expressed that way. My price is the
amount of writing I consider it worth my while to
do for the benefit of the possession of the clothes.
I may not even think of it in that way. I may be so
blinded to realities by little bits of paper that purport to be value that I never bother to work it out.
In that case I am a very poor judge of the national
accounts, and I doubt whether I ought to be
allowed to cast my vote in respect of a Budget.

Good, healthy, sound trade requires the presence
of a willing buyer and a willing seller. The buyer
will feel that the sacrifice demanded of him is not
more than he ought to make, and the seller will feel
in a general sort of way that the benefit which he
gets from making and selling is as much as he can
expect. But the willing buyer and the willing seller
both disappeared with the war, and their continued
absence is of much more importance to us than all
the discussions of the experts on inflation and
deflation. When Dr. Addison put it into our heads

that the proper price for war supplies was the cost of production plus a small percentage for overheads and management, he sowed the seeds of extravagance which have since multiplied a hundredfold. When Mr. Churchill, with scarcely more wisdom, added at a stroke $12\frac{1}{2}$ per cent. to everybody's wages, we parted company with the basic principles upon which economic safety and prosperity are dependent. In so far as any of us is endeavouring to perpetuate these artificial and unsound arrangements, we must each take a share of responsibility for the maintenance of an unsound position which will spoil our trade so long as it continues.

Inflation pushes prices up, and, while it lasts, is pleasant for everybody with anything to sell. Deflation is a more difficult and lengthy process, and produces hardships far more serious than the minor ills which tempted us to indulge in inflation. When, thanks to inflation, some of us have put ourselves into a position of unnatural advantage over the rest, we are not very willing to relinquish that advantage. When a $12\frac{1}{2}$ per cent. is freely distributed we all rush to get in, but when the reverse operation is necessary we all wait for somebody else to start. Even to-day, when large numbers are without the opportunity of earning a living, we find others still going on, by virtue of their political power, with inflationary processes, deliberately causing further damage to those who cannot get for themselves this sort of protection. But even if we do not strive to go on inflating, it is natural that we should struggle to avoid the hardships of deflation.

A trade union wage, a ring to maintain a market price, or a protective tariff, is very reluctantly abandoned. This troublesome task of getting back to the normal, with its necessary lowering of the standard for some of us, its bankruptcy for others, and its hardship for all in sheltered industries, causes millions of people quite naturally to search about for safety. It produces a scramble to get on to public funds, where alone is to be found a measure of immunity from the inconveniences of market conditions. Thousands of young men are to-day turning their attention to the public service because the attractions of a market which must go on falling until the last bit of inflation has gone are not strong enough for them. If a boy has to decide whether he will go into, say, the glove trade or try to get himself a job in a Government office, he needs a strong character to decide in favour of gloves. If he thinks the thing out at all, he will notice my position as a journalist or the position of any ordinary worker. He will see that while I can decline to pay an improper price for a pair of gloves, I cannot as a taxpayer decline to pay him £6 a week for counting and classifying rabbits in the Ministry of Agriculture. If, therefore, this boy can get into the Ministry of Agriculture, he would appear, in present circumstances, to be a good deal safer than doing useful work in the glove trade.

A normal state of affairs is that in which people generally feel that the value of things is measured with something approaching justice, and to-day very few people have that feeling. Our price list is

artificial, almost every figure having behind it some
official or unoffical forcing arrangement designed to
protect it from the healthy operation of natural
forces. The buyer of a guinea book knows that by an
artificial trade arrangement the bookseller is able to
secure to himself 7s. out of that guinea. This knowledge rankles in the mind of the buyer, and thus in
consequence leads to an unwillingness to buy books.
But when we examine the matter further, the sense
of injustice goes beyond the buyer to the unfortunate bookseller himself, who has to shoulder odium
as a profiteer, but knows quite well that a large
slice of his 7s. is taken from him in rates to pay, say,
the dustman, £4 10s. a week. The dustman, in his
turn, feels no injustice in his £4 10s., but he does
grumble when he discovers that his money is of far
less value to him because the railways arrange their
affairs in such a way as to double the price of his
coal. The railwayman reciprocates, and finds injustice in the fact that the dustman's wages represent a movement which doubles the Budget and
makes new and necessary capital for railways twice
as expensive. And so we get into a sort of vicious
circle. All are conscious of injustice, and not un-
naturally trade is bad. Prosperity, depending upon
confidence and a sense of right, will come back to
us only when we all have, on the whole, a feeling
that we are giving and getting value for value.

After twenty-five years of the new politics, in
which everybody has been scrambling for artificial
assistance of some kind or another, and the value
given has ceased to be a consideration with us, the

deflation process is peculiarly hard. It is much harder for us than for the French or the Austrians or the Germans. They had the advantage of an excursion into inflation in its simplest form, and know each of them from personal experience all its joys and its dangers. We have been inflating before and since the war in a more subtle, general, undefined sort of way. We do not recognise that we are in a thoroughly unhealthy and unnatural condition. We have no striking illustration like the " flight from the mark " to make clear to us the folly of our ways, and our road back to normality and stability is therefore the more difficult. We are, however, beginning to recognise that most of our recent actions are wrong. The state of the national finances and the number of the unemployed give all of us doubts. Even our politicians lack their usual confidence. We are beginning to see that adding one artificial arrangement to another, piling a new wrong on to an old one, finding palliatives instead of remedies for ills, will only lead us deeper into the morass.

To argue this way is not popular when some proposal is advanced for giving a few shillings a week to a widow or someone else who is the victim of political folly. But when that same sentimental desire to make everybody happy is applied to the case of a Prime Minister who finds that £5,000 a year is not sufficient to cover his expenses, then sentiment should give place to sense. The nation as a whole is called upon for sacrifice, suffering, and effort, to avert the collapse of society. Nothing less serious is in question. If we have really become so mad as to think that everything can be put right by increasing everybody's money, and we are going to start with the Prime Minister, then there is very little purpose in rendering an account or bothering about figures. We can make up our minds to eat, drink, and be merry, with full knowledge of the consequences.

But after more than five and twenty years of the new politics, during the whole of which time we have driven the trouble deeper and deeper, ceased to use the word economy, and altogether forgotten its meaning, there are happily signs that we are beginning to recognise the error of our ways. We must deflate down to normal, whatever the cost or the suffering, " normal " being, not some index figure calculated by the higher mathematicians, but a rate of exchange as between man and man which leaves both with a sense of right and justice and value given and received. In a sentence, not each according to his needs, but each according to his worth.

CHAPTER V

THE BILL

POSTERITY, *debtor to* POLITICS

	£
The War itself	7,000,000,000
Loss on Housing	500,000,000
Pensions	3,000,000,000
Unemployment Liability	200,000,000
Trade Facilities Guarantees and Subsidies, loss	75,000,000
Local Authorities' Debts, Inflation	250,000,000
Vested Interest in Public Expenditure ..	11,625,000,000

Say £20,000,000,000   Total :   £22,650,000,000
E. & O. (mostly O.) E.

There are two fairly recent experiences in the making up of accounts which can serve as guides in this endeavour to reduce to figures the effects of the political era 1900–30. Just as that era dawned, President Kruger presented a bill to Mr. Chamberlain in which he first brought it to our minds that mental and moral damage might be expressed in terms of figures. Nearly twenty years later the Peace Conference in Paris spent the best part of a year in making up a bill of costs against the defeated Germans. A study of Mr. Keynes's *The Economic Consequences of the Peace* will bring home to the reader the dangers and the difficulties of this sort of task. When we were promised that the German lemon would be squeezed until we

could hear the pips squeak, we were counting up
the fruits of victory in figures which at one
time reached the grotesquely fantastic total of
£250,000,000,000. When, after a long succession
of conferences and agreements, Dawes Plans and
Young Plans have been succeeded by further
necessary steps to sanity, we shall begin to realise
the folly of a political method which mistakes
figures for realities. We should therefore approach
our task with great humility, and with a full consciousness that when we speak of a pound we mean
something that is very different from the sovereign
of our grandfathers and may be still more different
from that of our grandchildren. Indeed, the importance which figures of this kind possess in themselves is not so great as the importance attaching
to the instability of their very nature. When, at
the beginning of the new political period, we
tacitly accepted the notion that it was right and
proper for politicians to handle large sums of
money for purposes strangely called "economic,"
we not only altered the character and quality of
money itself, but we cracked and weakened the
foundations upon which every individual in the
world had hitherto been able to build his own little
bits of security. By contrast to the South African
or Parisian method of making up an account, we
might accept as guiding principles the ideas which
are behind the numerous Companies Acts. Parliament in its wisdom has laid it down that the
business man must expose to the world all his
troubles, past, present, and future. He must make

it quite clear to everybody that he has no undisclosed liabilities. He must advertise to his creditors everything in the nature of a contingent risk. Much good might be done if the Chancellor of the Exchequer were obliged to conform to the requirements which the law puts upon the business man. In that case provision would have to be made in the annual Budget for immense sums, the eventual cost of contractual obligations which the sovereign power of that abstract entity the State is supposed to be able to honour out of means which the future will provide. The reader will notice that the little account of rather more than £20,000,000,000 in seven simple items is marked in the merchant's manner, "errors and omissions excepted." It pretends to be nothing more than a sample of a much longer and a much bigger account. The errors are no doubt very big – some will think on the side of over-statement; I take leave to think on the side of under-statement. On this question I again refer the reader to *The Economic Consequences of the Peace* as a lucid and interesting illustration of the difficulties in calculating at all in figures of such magnitude. But figures being only indications of movement in more important things, if they only put a doubt into the minds of our 30,000,000 electors as to the wisdom of the road along which political activity is leading us, it does not very much matter if there is a 20 or 30 per cent. error one way or the other.

We start with the costs of the war because the £7,000,000,000 is a matter of record. It should, however, be noted in passing that this vast sum differs in its essence from a debt incurred in respect of value received. We have in an economic sense nothing whatever to show for it – no remnant, no dividend, out of this £7,000,000,000. On the contrary, we know that we must add to the figure an equal or larger sum if we include the accumulated treasure which we blew away on the battlefields, treasure which, but for the war, would have remained in existence for the benefit of posterity.

£7,000,000,000 is a self-flattering under-estimate of the load of effort we are leaving our children to carry. The figure represents the sum this generation has borrowed from the past and paid to itself for work done during the war. It should be examined by us, as it will undoubtedly be examined by future generations, who will find the figures to have a different meaning. As a sample of the whole, consider a pair of army boots, down in the bill as worth £2. These same boots were made and sold by us before the war for half the money, and the price of them will some day again approach the pre-war figure. The people who will pay this £7,000,000,000 will have to make two pairs of boots to satisfy the price of one pair made by us, and every other item in the bill has something of the same character about it. The coming generation are confronted, by our extravagance, with the double task of rendering proper value for value to themselves and replacing with real values our inflated wastage.

The £7,000,000,000 takes no account of war pensions, neither does it include the economic loss arising from the killing of millions of our best men, who were thus robbed of the chance to make their contribution to the economic progress of mankind.

We have charged in our account £500,000,000 in respect of losses on housing, a round figure which is probably very much under the mark. We arrive at it from the knowledge that since the war some 1,500,000 new houses have been erected, and we calculate an ultimate loss of £330 per house. The Statistical Abstract for 1927 admits to liabilities outstanding against local authorities on housing in England and Wales alone of £320,000,000. The figures for Scotland and Ireland are not separately shown, so the total is more. The liabilities of local authorities, however, do not include the vast sums contributed by the Exchequer and remaining as part of the National Debt. Putting national and local debt together, there is certainly not less than £500,000,000 of housing in it. But in making up posterity's account, we have to take note of all the old buildings sold at inflated values. Many of us of this generation are guilty of taking the solid £1,000 worth of bricks and mortar bequeathed to us by previous generations, selling it for £2,000 or £3,000, squandering the difference in high living or taxation, and leaving the higher false book value for our children to depreciate and write off. In putting the financial troubles of the future at £500,000,000 in respect of housing we are certainly under-estimating. If in the Kruger or the Lloyd George manner we cared to consider the damage done to the future by our failure to maintain and develop the housing property of the nation at the rate that was bequeathed to us as a tradition by those who lived between 1850 and 1900, then posterity has a still longer bill against us under this head.

Leaving the consideration of pensions to another chapter and passing to unemployment benefit, so wrongly called insurance, we have put the liability down at the comparatively modest figure of £200,000,000. It will indeed be a fortunate circumstance if the nation extracts itself from this unemployment complication for so small a sum. The position at the moment is that a married man with three children, having paid 17s. 6d. in what we call insurance, is entitled by law to £118 in benefit, and by the custom of the moment to as much more as he appears to need. The prostitution of the word insurance is another little vanity which will not add to our credit with posterity. Insurance used to mean a payment calculated on an actuarial basis to cover a risk carefully measured on the assumption that every insured would do his very utmost to avoid that risk. We insure our lives, and henceforth exert every endeavour to avoid a claim. Indeed, we look forward with delight to living long enough to make a loss on our insurance contract. We insure against fire, and get up in the middle of the night because the wife thinks she notices a smell

of burning. The essence of insurance, properly
understood, is that the insured can be relied upon
to go to extremes to avoid becoming a charge
upon the funds. To apply the word to a system
which is rapidly pauperising a large section of the
nation is a glaring instance of the misuse of language. The insurance fund, as we write, is admittedly in debt – £60,000,000. That account is made
up, as the State makes up all its accounts, without
any true actuarial or accountancy basis. If this insurance were placed in the hands of a genuine insurance institution, enormous reserves would be
required by Act of Parliament to cover the liabilities which are known to exist. Contractual obligations are made with millions of people who are
entitled to look for cover, but whose cover in
this case consists of nothing but the willingness
of the taxpayer of the future to pay. The sum
of £200,000,000 is certainly a far too moderate
figure to cover the burden we are handing to
future generations on account of our folly in this
matter.

It is very difficult to arrive at an exact figure to
indicate the liabilities created under the felicitous
subterfuges known as Trade Facilities Guarantees
and Subsidies. There is no difference between a
subsidy and a guarantee. In the one case you pay
to go in, and in the other you pay to come out.
Many years ago Disraeli parted company with
national tradition when he made the State a shareholder in the Suez Canal. That little gamble has
paid us handsomely if considered by itself, but in

so far as it was a precedent and has formed the excuse for State-dabbling in oil, in ships, in beet sugar, and in many other ways, we have paid very heavily for it. The published accounts, which are a long way behind the times, admit to guarantees given to a number of scheduled undertakings covering a sum of £150,000,000. We have yet to learn what additions have been made by the present Government in guaranteeing payment for the supply of goods to Russia. Posterity will have to write down by scores of millions the capital of undertakings floated during this mad period with Government support because no private capital could face the risk. One illustration indicates the character of numerous transactions. At a time when we were subsidising wages in existing coalfields in order to save a great industry ruined by the peace treaty, we actually put on to the national liabilities guarantees of principal and interest for the sinking of further coal-mines in Kent. Volumes would be required to enumerate all the things done in a single year since the war to weaken the economic position of posterity. Every day produces its quota of unnecessary extravagance, some of it large, some of it small, but all equally bad. For instance, as I write, Mr. Lansbury announces that he will cancel the lease of the Royal Zoological Society, open the Zoo to the public, and put it on to public funds. Thus the Exchequer, instead of receiving a small rent to help it with its obligations, will shoulder the cost of the Zoo, a cost which in a very few years will be swollen out of recognition.

The visitor will save 6*d*., and the taxpayer will pay half a crown. This seemingly small extravagance can be multiplied ten thousand times by reference to the records of our thousands of local authorities all of whom have indulged in something of this kind during the last few years. Everywhere we find that private economy has been sacrificed to public extravagance.

Another example is furnished by the British Industries Fair, which costs the Exchequer £25,000 a year in advertising alone and much more in other ways, whereas before it was established substantial sums were paid in Income Tax from numerous privately-run exhibitions and fairs. If trade returns are any criterion, these private fairs were much more beneficial to our commerce and industry. In big and little things alike, we have forgotten the meaning of economy.

Wages are paid in every railway service as compensation for a cost-of-living index figure, and Acts of Parliament lay it down that railway companies can charge rates for freight which simply drive consignors to find other and cheaper means of transport. The minor industries have been afflicted with the same disease.

The future will think little of us who have taken 45,000,000 British citizens, possessed of the finest economic heritage in the world, and set up before them false gods in the shape of economic rights; who have presented the world with the appalling spectacle of millions of paupers receiving their compassionate allowance, for that is what it really amounts to, and cherishing a grievance because they believe themselves to be possessed of rights which should make the dole still more. The new politics has afflicted us with two big new classes unworthy of the name of citizens – the tax-dodgers and the dole-drawers. Millions of men and women whose minds might be used for good economic purposes are driven by sheer necessity to give their effort and intelligence, on the one hand to evading the oppressive demands of the State, and on the other hand to making larger claims upon it.

The sixth figure in our account is merely a token to represent the vast depreciation which the rate-payers of the future will have to face in respect of municipal enterprises undertaken with the aid of borrowed money in a market where all values were double the normal.

The last item in our little bill presents more difficulties. The figure is calculated in a very simple way. We have assumed that in pursuance of a new spirit of economy it is possible to reduce our public expenditure by £25,000,000 a year. We have set out on this course with the object of making our rates and taxes no heavier than those which afflict other industrial countries except America. We have not thought it possible that the English within a measurable distance of time will take the saner view of their American cousins, and we therefore allow double the public expenditure per head of the population as compared with the United States. On this basis a simple calculation will show that we should require thirty

ER

years to accomplish these aims, and that in the meantime we shall have to disburse in uneconomic rates and taxes the sum set down in our bill of £11,625,000,000. This amount of uncovered liability is at the moment growing very rapidly, and will grow every day that we continue upon our present course.

Considering, therefore, only the items set out in the account with which we started this chapter, our national liabilities approach very nearly to the enormous sum of £500 per head of the population, and this is the side of the matter which I desire to stress. It will be obvious to anyone who has followed the argument so far that there is any amount of room for difference of opinion on detail. The figure £500 may be an over-estimate or an under-estimate. Technicians and experts might sit for years and argue, and still differ as to the exact figure. We do know, however, that before we embarked upon the war the total national and local liabilities amounted to no more than £18 per head of the population. It is beyond dispute that the child who was born a British citizen in July, 1914, came into the world committed to shoulder this modest burden. Neither can it be denied that the child who first sees the light in the year 1930 must be prepared, if he does no more than his fair share in the acceptance of economic responsibility, to face a burden which is vastly in excess of £18. If the £500 that we have considered is divided by three, he still has nine times as much economic trouble on his tender shoulders as the pre-war child.

An expert examination of our financial position would take account not only of the liabilities created by actions already taken, but would also have to note liabilities arising from those impolitic pronouncements which the politicians call policies. If Sir William Plender were appointed liquidator on behalf of the nation, he would find it necessary to make some provision against the risk of the various political programmes which threaten us. For example, the Trades Union Congress goes on pressing its demand for State pensions of 30s. a week for all at sixty. A Socialist Government will be quite unable to avoid a claim from such a quarter indefinitely. The Treasury has calculated that 25s. a week would cost £330,000,000 in 1930, rising to £495,000,000 by 1960, but the Treasury only deals with one year at a time. If we can imagine that such a burden were placed with a regular insurance institution and proper provision to meet it were thus made, we can get a reliable estimate of the weight of the liability. The tables of rates vary slightly, but an annuity for a man of sixty is worth about fifteen years' purchase, and at the lower 1930 figure the trade union demand therefore represents a capital liability of no less than £4,950,000,000 for pensions at 25s. to men and women who are now sixty years of age, or £6,000,000,000 if the rate is to be 30s. Seeing, however, that the liability is perpetual and increasing, thirty years' purchase would hardly cover it, and the proper capital value is in the neighbourhood of £12,000,000,000.

The Independent Labour Party should amend its motto and make it read, " Socialism in *our* time and starvation for our children," for that is what it really means. Considering, as we are endeavouring to do, the duty of one generation to another, this pension proposition appears to be the meanest and most cowardly of all the new political proposals. The Trades Union Congress is not devoid of decent feeling and a sense of right, and nothing but a blind political fanaticism, which will certainly pass away, can explain the extraordinary spectacle of a powerful body of healthy men, most of them with a group of charming children at home, calmly voting to themselves pensions which a moment's reflection is sufficient to show must wreck the economic position of those children.

The deliberations of any number of Royal Commissions and experts which might reduce our £500 in respect of the seven items of our little account would still have to reckon with a great many other unpaid bills representing delights that we of this generation have thought well to enjoy and have forgotten to pay for.

There is a side to this problem to which all too little consideration appears to be given. Public expenditure on the present unprecedented scale is rendered possible by the existence of taxable private wealth accumulated when public demands were much lower. The steady weakening of the position of the private owner which has proceeded in recent years, even if it satisfies the views of those who object to private wealth, has certainly weakened our capacity to collect taxes. The problem of the future would therefore appear to be, not how to increase taxation, but rather how to maintain private resources at a level which will be adequate to provide for the most modest estimate of the tax needs of the coming years.

Consider the private affairs of a family, and notice the difference in them between 1913 and 1930. The child who, in 1913, inherited a house built in solid fashion at 1880 prices, even though it had been left with a mortgage up to the full two-thirds of its value, was in a perfectly safe position. He really came into tangible property, and could consider himself under an obligation to his forbears. By contrast, the child who in 1930 inherits a house shoddily and flimsily built at 1925 prices, with a State-supported mortgage up to 90 per cent. of its inflated value, is bankrupt. That child inherits, not an estate, but a liability. If from the simple case of a house we move on to a wider range of property, the bill grows out of knowledge. It cannot surely be disputed that the progress of civilisation depends upon the care and wisdom with which one generation will accept the savings of the past, preserve them, add to them, and pass them on to the next. From this point of view our successors as British citizens have to face all the painful cost of wiping out all the inflation of recent years. They will have to pay for all the de-rationalising, if I may invent a term, the necessity for which will presently become apparent. They will have to write down buildings, stocks, machinery,

and suffer all the loss from a market which must
go on falling until we reach something that will be
recognised as normal. Posterity is not likely to
draw a fine distinction between public debts
and private debts. It will not matter to our grandchildren whether the cause of the lower standard of
life forced upon them by us is rates and taxes or
private financial folly. The two things go together
and are inextricably mixed up. Consider the case
of an estate or a business passing from one generation to the next. Take the owner who has the good
fortune to follow a careful proprietor. He will find
that a conservative policy has been followed in
the calculation of profits. He will discover that a
good part of those profits has been put back into
the business. He will not fail to be thankful that
the capital account has been kept as low as possible, and he will derive great benefits from valua-
tions of stock and other assets made on a safe,
sound basis. The future of that man will be an easy
one. If, however, a management has systematically
over-estimated income and dissipated profits on
unproductive purposes such as taxes, has made
inadequate reserves, has written up the capital account and over-valued the stocks and buildings,
then the beneficiaries will inherit nothing but
worry and difficulty. The amount of trouble which
we who have lived through the period of the new
politics are handing on to the future is incapable
of arithmetical calculation. We can only get
glimpses of it ; we can only form rough ideas. But
a glimpse is enough and an idea sufficient to make

us very sure that as a generation we are making no contribution to progress. The political damage to our economic position can be illustrated if we examine the circumstances of an individual business from another point of view. Let us suppose that "A" is possessed of a business which is honestly worth £100,000, and in the year 1927 or 1928 he takes stock of his position. At the top of the list of his contingent liabilities he writes :

Death Duties £20,000

and he knows that his family will be left with a business worth £80,000. But the £100,000 is in buildings, machinery, stock, and book debts, and probably requires supporting with a bank loan. The business is quite unable to write a cheque for £20,000. So that "A" knows that when his end comes his family will be left with all the difficulties of finding in cash, somehow or another, a sum which represents two or three years' gross income. Mortgages will have to be arranged or other devices adopted. Having these facts in mind, "A," say in 1928, notices that the speculative and inflationary public opinion, created by the political mind applied to industrial affairs, values his business at a very much higher figure. He therefore succumbs to the temptation to sell it to a company promoter for £200,000, puts that sum into Government stocks and retires upon the income. When death overtakes him the family will pay death-duties of £48,400 and be left with gilt-edged securities of £151,600. The whole thing is very regrettable, but no one will fail to understand or to sympathise with "A's" point of view. Out of this comparatively simple transaction all sorts of complications arise. The State will appear to have made an immediate profit of £28,400, for it has received in figures written on pieces of paper £48,400 in death-duties instead of the £20,000 to which it was previously entitled. But in the end the State will pay through the nose for this illusory profit. It undertakes an obligation to pay 5 per cent. upon £151,600 worth of War Loan which, when Government credit returns, as some day or another it must return, to, let us say, a 3 per cent. basis, will represent a liability of £252,000. In the meantime the public, who have bought "A's" business in 1928 for £200,000, have sold the shares to another public, all bitten with the inflationary fever germinated by Government extravagance, for £400,000. Some of these people will in the meantime pay death-duties; all of them will pay income tax on exaggerated profits which have no reality except in microscopic atoms of ink written upon paper, and then, still a little later on, a third public, in so far as these shares have been handed about on the market, will have to write off the bulk of the values which they vainly hoped to have acquired. All this mass of trouble, ending most probably in the break-up of the business itself, arises from the simple circumstance that "A" tried to accommodate his affairs to the impossible demands of a stupid State that imagined it was

serving the public interest by confiscating private
capital.

Thus it will be seen that if the real account which
we are preparing for the disadvantage of posterity
could be written up and audited, the sum of
£20,000,000,000 with which we started is a mere
indication of a much larger figure.

As against this sort of argument, it may be said
that in the meantime our standard of living has
improved. No one who has experienced life in a
place like the East End of London for half a
century can doubt that the condition of the people
as a whole, in such matters as clothes and food and
general material well-being, is better in 1930 than
it was in 1880. There are those who take some
comfort in this fact; who, unable to comprehend
the bigger economic movements which we have
been considering, say to themselves that all these
complications will somehow come right, and that
in the meantime poverty has diminished and life
is happier. This leads me to enquire, putting the
matter in the simplest way, whether the Romans
in the luxurious days of the second or third century
were conscious of the fact that they were ruining
their Empire or the civilisation that it represented,
or whether any civilisation that has gone under
has done so consciously. The history of Rome under
Marcus Aurelius bears many resemblances to our
history under politicians of the social reform
type.[1] If we arrive at the opinion that the rise in
the standard of living which is obvious in a place

[1] *See* Appendix V.

like Whitechapel is likely to be of a temporary nature, that we are laying up trouble which will bring Whitechapel far below its Victorian position, or even that we are failing to make provision for a still better standard of life in that place, then we must accuse ourselves of failure as a generation to make our contribution to the advance of mankind. Let us return to the family analogy, for, while these problems become unwieldy from a national point of view, they are simplicity itself if the nation can be considered as a bigger edition of the family. Nothing is easier than for any family to live upon its capital. Whether that capital be large or small makes no difference. The man with £100 in the Post Office Savings Bank, and earning £3 a week as a railway servant, can put 60 per cent. on to his standard of living for a year by the simple process of spending his £100 within that period, and enjoying all the delights which come from an expenditure of £5 a week. If, as a nation, we are doing anything of that kind to-day, we are providing for the downfall of our children.

"If the State could examine its conscience every night, in the absence of all flatterers, and in that privacy which is unfortunately denied to it, surely it would become conscious of the fact that it has many defects, that its nature is full of contradictions and incoherences, that its paramount duty is to cultivate prudence and reserve, and to limit its action to what is strictly indispensable. So far from this, however, the Modern State is as full of presumption as children are, or conquerors; those by whom it is manned wage ever a desperate struggle, which is constantly renewing itself; they have all the pride and consciousness of triumph, and all the impassioned eagerness of men who feel that they have only a precarious tenure of power."[1]

[1] *The Modern State*: Professor Pierre Leroy Beaulieu.

CHAPTER VI

LIABILITY FOR PENSIONS

PROPHECY is a risky business, but it is not necessary to be a prophet to point with full knowledge and complete accuracy to some of the things which are bound to happen in the future. When a bill is accepted it is safe to prophesy that the drawer will expect to receive payment on the date named in the document. We know with certainty that on June 1st, 1947, £2,184,468,777 of 5 per cent. War Loan falls due for payment. We know that hundreds of thousands of us have put our savings, large and small, into this figure with perfect confidence that the money will be forthcoming without any sort of question on June 1st, 1947. We know, further, of the vital importance to all of us, to the pauper in receipt of relief no less than the millionaire holder of big blocks of War Loan, of maintaining inviolate the assurance that this huge sum is absolutely certain of payment in some form or another which will be recognised as equally valuable on the date named seventeen years hence.

Examining the matter more carefully, we begin to see that our discharge of this huge liability can only be made in a convenient way by cultivating, maintaining, and improving the general confidence in public credit, so that holders of this loan, or others with savings to invest, may be willing to accept in its place new securities in which they will have an equal faith. The aim of every Chancellor of the Exchequer is to fund loan. That is to say, he tries to get the investing public to accept the view that State credit is good for all time, and some Chancellor of the future will, or so it is assumed, have the good fortune to find such a healthy state of public opinion that investors will come forward and say: "We will leave this £2,000,000,000 in the hands of the State for all time, for we have complete confidence that the State will for all time pay the agreed rate of interest upon it." If by our political actions we do anything to weaken the steady growth of this confidence in the State, then, when the first of June, 1947, arrives, the investing public will decline to renew the loan except for a shorter period at a higher rate of interest.

This is not a question of capitalism or socialism. It is not even a question of opinion. The facts are quite clear. We have to-day £2,184,468,777 of value, and if we fail to maintain that value then the holders of the loan lose their money and, still more serious, the State loses its credit, and its ability to function for the benefit of all weakens and disappears. In considering this great question we have as business men to recognise that for the time being anything in the nature of the paying off of loans has been reduced to a farce. We have arranged our daily expenditure on such a liberal scale that there is no margin to do more than a very nominal amount of debt repayment. We therefore depend for our solvency and our ability to carry on upon the maintenance intact and the gradual improvement of our credit, enabling us year by year, as personal savings become available, to fund or perpetuate more and more of our debt. In twelve years since the termination of the war we have amassed a funded debt amounting to no more than £1,478,287,690. This, however, is an exaggeration, because we had a funded debt of nearly half the amount before we entered into the war, so that in twelve years we have rid ourselves of the inconvenient obligation of meeting short-dated loans only to the extent of about one-fifteenth of the total national and local obligations. Considering only the national figures of recognised debt, and ignoring much bigger liabilities which for our purposes we put into the Account Rendered, it will take at the present rate not less than 150 years before the Treasury, the money market, and the tiny little savings of the smallest of us, are free from the risk of disturbance and depreciation due to the existence of fourteen-fifteenths of our enormous liabilities, some of which will every few months be presented as a bill to be paid on the spot.

So far as our troubles are due to the war it is very little use to argue about them, but so far as these same troubles are due to post-war political folly we should strive to understand them and strive to make what amends are in our limited powers. Some of our political reformers must feel occasional pangs of conscience when they reflect on the results of their endeavour to relieve the poorer classes of that incubus, the idle rich. The present position is that one section of the nation is in a condition of perpetual slavery to another section who own the eight or ten thousand millions of public debt. This slavery, on consideration, proves to be far worse than any other sort of economic slavery, because any suggestion that it is wrong, or that it should be altered, repudiated, or abolished, involves the destruction of the national credit, and with it the destruction of all hope of a continuance of such national social services as are wise, or the development of any such new services as may seem from time to time desirable. It was easy enough thirty years ago for reformers to talk about despoiling dukes. It is not nearly so easy for the same sort of optimists boldly to suggest the abolition of the national credit.

If, however, our consideration of the national obligations is limited to the amount of the National Debt and to the possibilities or the difficulties of funding and of payment, we are grossly underestimating the size of the burdens placed by us upon the shoulders of the workers of the future. It is high time that we took notice of an oppressive new liability to which day by day we are adding, if not with complete ignorance of its existence, at least without due regard to its importance. It is a tradition of the public service that employment is continuous, and that such employment carries with it the right to a pension. This tradition has great value, and is amply worth maintaining. When men or women with a high standard of education,

and a deep sense of the honour and distinction attaching to right forms of public service, are prepared to give themselves to such necessary work
as should be performed by the Treasury, the Home
Office, the Foreign Office, or in the administration
of justice or the provision of defence, it is in every
way desirable that the State should make it clear
to such persons that in undertaking this sort of
necessary duty they need entertain no fears as to
their own personal financial needs now or in the
future. It is very much to the credit of the genuine
Civil Service that they have as a class been willing
to allow the benefits of this honourable and proper
tradition to extend beyond the normal departments of genuine government and to embrace
every Tom, Dick, and Harry who within recent
years has been able to wangle himself into one or
other of the innumerable public offices which have
sprung up like mushrooms during and since the
war, and which will, when sanity returns, be swept
off to the rubbish-heap.

In the meantime, however, we of this generation
have heaped on to posterity an enormous liability in
the shape of pensions, and we cannot find in the
public accounts any effort to estimate the amount
of this liability, any attempt to provide for it, or
any desire to regulate or to limit it. The following
tables, admittedly incomplete, indicate that our
payments to persons in the enjoyment of pensions
in the year 1930 are certainly not less than
£115,000,000.

NATIONAL AND LOCAL PENSIONS

TABLE I.—NATIONAL

	1914–15 £000	1927–8 £000	1928–9 £000	1929–30 £000
Pensions charged on Defence Votes	6,966	16,664	16,819	17,035
Pensions charged on Revenue Votes (excluding Post Office)	637	671	925	887
Civil Service Pensions (including Consolidated Fund Pensions)	887	1,803	1,799	1,803
War Pensions (including Merchant Seamen's Pensions and Administration)	—	61,877	57,627	54,114
Old Age Pensions	10,111	32,746	33,647	35,497
Payment to Widows', Orphans', and Old Age Contributory Pensions	—	4,000	4,000	4,000
Irish Police Pensions	448	700	696	701
State Payments in respect of :				
Police Pensions[1]	340	2,354	2,464	2,478
School Teachers' Pensions	244	2,140	1,007	1,512
TOTAL :	19,633	122,955	118,984	118,027

[1] Included in local police pensions. *See* table following.

FR

TABLE II.—LOCAL (*England and Wales*)

	1926–7 £000	1927–8 £000
London County Council	205	294
Metropolitan Borough Councils (including the City of London)	172	198
Metropolitan Water Board	36	33
Port of London Authority	231	242.5
City of London Police	120	126
Metropolitan Police	1,614	1,720
Poor Law Authorities (Metropolitan Asylums Board, Boards of Guardians, etc.)	509	589
County Borough Councils	363	438.5
County Councils (excluding L.C.C.)	37	Not available
County Police	1,192	1,259
Borough Councils	24	Not available
Borough Police	1,270	1,338
Urban District Councils	23	}Not available
Rural District Councils	1	
Miscellaneous (Parish Councils, Parish Meetings, Joint Boards, etc.)	8	
TOTAL :	5,805	

This money is paid out to persons who very properly regard their pensions as inviolable, and it represents a definite capital liability. Suppose, for instance, that the State were to approach an insurance company and ask them to take over the obligation to pay £115,000,000 a year. Such a company would probably capitalise this sum at thirty-three years' purchase – 3 per cent. at least. It must be remembered that the liability is a perpetual one, for any decrease in one class of pension will be balanced by increases in others. The liability will further tend to increase as the expectation of life increases, and if, taking all these matters into consideration, the sum is capitalised on a 3 per cent. basis, we find that there exists now a capital liability of £3,833.⅓ millions in respect of pensions at rates no heavier than the rates and amounts now payable. It must, however, be borne in mind that a public servant in receipt of a pension to-day was doing his public service many years ago. Roughly speaking, the retired Civil Servant of to-day entered upon his work not later than, say, 1905. Most of our Civil Service pensioners will have had five and twenty years of service to their credit; many of them will have had a great deal more. Thus it transpires that pensions paid to-day to public servants are really payments in respect of appointments which were made twenty or thirty or forty years ago. We have therefore to consider, if this liability rests upon us in respect of appointments made by our fathers, what sort of liability we are putting upon our children in respect of similar appointments made by us. We can get a glimpse of the probable course of events by glancing backwards. In 1914 our Old Age and Civil Service pensions cost less than £20,000,000 a year. If that liability had been capitalised upon the basis here suggested, there existed in 1914 a capital obligation of £666,000,000 in respect of these pensions. Sixteen years have therefore been sufficient to multiply this capital liability no less than six times.

Going back to 1905, when the liability for most of these pensions first arose, we discover that there were not more than one-third in number of the Civil Servants whom we now think we require to carry on the business of a modern Government. We also notice that the rates of pay for the various grades in 1905 gave roughly half the figures which are now considered appropriate. A simple calculation tells us that with three times the number and twice the pay we have a capital liability six times as heavy as that which attached to the Civil Service in 1905. If, therefore, we are right in assuming that the £3,833,000,000 is properly chargeable to the appointments of 1905, we may say that the ultimate capital liability for pension rights created by the new politics is something in the neighbourhood of £23,000,000,000. The reader who has followed the argument so far will be quick to notice that nearly half of the figure on which we based our calculations is represented by war pensions, which is a diminishing item, and in these impressive calculations no credit has been taken for the ultimate extinction of pensions arising out of the Great War. It must, however, be remembered that the provisions recently made for widows' and old age pensions will for many years to come absorb all the savings on war pensions and more, and it should further be remembered that, failing a rapid change in public opinion on these matters, these social pensions are likely to increase still further.

Calculations on such matters and in such figures are admittedly speculative in character. For instance, considerable differences in opinion are possible on such a question as whether pensions should be capitalised at 3 or $3\frac{1}{2}$ per cent., or whether the proper figure is 4 per cent. But, making the most generous allowances for differences such as these, it cannot be doubted that there exists a liability in respect of pensions which the whole of a year's income of all the people would be insufficient to discharge.

This is a liability from which we cannot escape. No one would suggest that the public pledge given to some aged Whitehall messenger or to the widow of a deceased workman should be withdrawn, repudiated, or modified. It represents an enormous burden upon us and upon our children. It means that another big slice of our production for the next forty or fifty years is handed over in advance to a big class of non-producers. It represents another bit of slavery for the workers of the future. Still, it cannot be avoided, and no one would desire to dishonour this existing obligation. It does, however, put a very grave responsibility upon us to pause and consider before creating further liabilities of this kind. When, for example,

Miss Bondfield goes out of her way to lower the standard of examination in order to swell still further the numerous staff of the Ministry of Labour, we ought, in deference to our own self-respect and in justice to our children, to recognise here and now that Miss Bondfield has added another few millions to this oppressive total.

However moderate an estimate we care to make on account of our pension policy, it is evident that our charges for pensions alone will in a very few years be heavier than the total charges for the service of our war debt.

CHAPTER VII

AM I PAYING MY WAY?

THE old economists based their wisdom on the belief that there existed something which may be called the Economic Man, and it is often argued against them that that belief was false, that man is not an economic creature, and that the average human being is not actuated by a conscious desire to regulate his life on a sound economic basis. This may be so if we are really determined to take as serious a good deal of the complicated rubbish which now passes for economic science. It is certainly absurd to imagine that forty million people or more can possess a perfect and expert knowledge of all the forces which contribute to their material well-being, or that each of them can or will act so as to contribute something hourly or daily to the general good. We are, however, drifting into a very dangerous condition if we accept the view that economics is an abstruse science the knowledge of which is reserved for the highbrows and the experts. A much healthier view, and one which is in better accord with the spirit of democracy, would hold that economic development in its broadest aspect is really a very simple matter capable of a rough understanding by everybody, and that an educated democratic people can be so instructed as to be capable of producing the best economic results from their everyday actions. Any other opinion cuts at the roots of democratic aspirations, makes rubbish of the notion that we can govern ourselves, and puts the nation and the world right into the hands of the newest and the worst of the dangers to civilisation – the experts.

We live by doing all sorts of things for others. Unless we are living on a small allotment subsisting on our own potatoes and keeping our own pig, we are working to produce something which others require. Having done our work, we proceed to exchange our product for the product of others. In so far as that exchange is free and unfettered, we tend always to receive the maximum of the product of others in return for such services as we can render. That is, stated very simply and briefly, the basis upon which civilisation has developed. If we make that basis clear to our people they will for the most part act in a sensible way, and the Economic Man will be a very common reality amongst us. If, on the other hand, we pursue the course now popular, and lead our children to believe that 9d. can be secured for 4d., or that there is anything economic in the notion " Each according to his needs," then, of course, the Economic Man will most certainly disappear. There are few elementary school children incapable of understanding the problem of wealth if only we will begin with simple realities. Even the higher mathematician finds it necessary to acquire a knowledge of addition and subtraction and the multiplication table. But in the modern economics the method is different. We ignore simple things and invite our beginners to discuss the theory of surplus, trade balances, currencies or the intricacies of taxation.

In *The Confessions of a Capitalist* I endeavoured to work out a complicated theory with a dozen tennis balls and again with a simple shovelful of sand. Those illustrations, if I may judge from the correspondence of the last few years, have been helpful to not a few people. For my present purpose let us assume that the only commodity which man requires for his complete well-being is a potato; visualise a society, such as ours, on an island and requiring only some one thing. A potato does as well for the purpose as anything else. Let us pile up all the potatoes in a heap in the middle of the island, which is in effect what is done to-day by the rather more convenient process of registering their value in the Bankers' Clearing House. It will be quite obvious even to a child that if the society eats more potatoes than it grows, its wealth, considered as a whole, is diminishing. If, on the other hand, season by season, rather more potatoes are added to the pile than are taken off it, the wealth of the society is increasing. Coming to the next stage, everyone will see that if an individual eats potatoes and puts no fresh ones on to the pile, that individual is a charge on society. If another individual grows and puts on to the pile just as many potatoes as he eats, then he is paying his way and is neither a profit nor a loss to the rest. Lastly, the man who grows more potatoes than he eats is doing something to build up the total wealth of the society. We have spent so much time squabbling as to the individual ownership of the potatoes, deceiving ourselves as to who exactly was responsible for their production, thinking of them as personal property rather than as common wealth, that most of us have lost this conception of the mass. If the mass diminishes, then its ownership becomes correspondingly less important. There is, of course, ample room for difference of opinion in all the little details that multiply as civilisation advances, concerning ownership, distribution, and the relative position of individual members of any society. But if we discuss all these matters with something like the heap of potatoes at the back of our minds, our discussion is likely to have an element of sense about it. If each of our actions were tested by its effect upon the total wealth, most of our political programmes would be recognised as wealth destroyers. Even the best political effort relieves half a crown's worth of poverty in one quarter by destroying five shilling's worth of wealth in another.

We should have a nation composed entirely of economic men if every man would subject himself to a little catechism about each of his wants and actions: "Am I paying my way? Have I really paid for the dinner I have eaten or the clothes I have put on ? My dinner and my clothes represent effort, work, expenditure, the creation of wealth by various other people. I take that wealth out of a common stock. If I am satisfied that I have myself created wealth, put forward effort, or performed work, of a value equal to the dinner or the clothes, then the community considered as a whole is no worse off on my account, and I can find some pleasure in the thought that I am paying my way. If I have these things in mind, I may be called an economic man. If, when I ask myself these questions, I am forced to admit that I have given less value than I get, I must also admit that the world in an economic sense is the poorer because I am in it. If on the other hand I am able to feel that I have really given better value in my product, whatever it may be, than I have received in the shape of a dinner or a suit of clothes, then the world is the richer for my presence in it, and I may call myself in truth a civilisation builder. The heap of potatoes is bigger because I am there."

Most of the people, what might perhaps be called the middle economic class, will be content to feel that they are paying their way, holding their own, constituting a charge on nobody, and accepting no responsibility for others. A minority of any society of people will possess that progressive spirit which will force them to be civilisation builders, and they will always give a little more than they get. Another section of the people, some from misfortune, some from folly, and, to-day, many more from political falsehood, will always be unable to give a satisfactory answer to the question "Am I paying my way?" and will always absorb some of the surplus created by the second class. In so far as this third class are the victims of misfortune that could not be avoided and incapacity which cannot be cured, then, on the principle which leads us to adjust the burden of taxation to the ability of the taxpayer, the second class must, in the interests of society as a whole, make up the deficiency of the third.

Thanks to a quarter of a century of active damage from the new politics, we have diminished the second class and developed the third, and the heap of potatoes is day by day shrinking in consequence. The new politics treats the second class as profiteers and thieves and puts in their way month by month fresh obstructions, thus limiting their necessary activities. At the same time it is foolish enough to flatter and indulge the third class, and thus make as certain as politics can that the common stock shall diminish as rapidly as possible. Ignoring for the moment all the contentious complications which admittedly arise out of this simple argument, few will be found to deny the wisdom of the suggestion that day by day each citizen should ask himself the question "Am I paying my way?" The outstanding difference between America and England is that the American does in fact put that question to himself, while the Englishman hardly gives it a thought. The perfect civilisation will emerge when we produce a people with the English character and the American economic sense.

If the reader, having this question in mind, will look about him and consider the first thing that is at hand, a number of considerations quite new to many of us will come to his mind. He is, for instance, reading these lines in a house which, let us say, is the product of 8,000 hours of skilled work on the part of bricklayers, carpenters, masons, plasterers, architects, and the rest. Has he paid for it? Has he contributed to the wealth existing in the country something that will balance up with the 8,000 hours of others' work represented by the house that he is enjoying? As he examines the matter carefully, he will notice that he is not called upon to balance the whole of the 8,000 hours. The house, if it was built before the Addison-Wheatley period, will last rather longer than the reader, and others who will use it may therefore be expected to pay part of its cost. It is obvious that the bricklayers, carpenters, masons, plasterers, and architects, who put 8,000 hours' work into this house did so because they hoped to establish claims on an equal amount of work performed by the man who was to use the house or, thanks to the civilising complications of money, on other sorts of producers. If, gentle reader, you are the tenant of a council house, for which you are paying 9s. 6d. a week rent while the bricklayers, carpenters, masons, and plasterers, have found it necessary to draw another £1 a week from the ratepayers or the taxpayers to balance the account, then you are not paying your way. It may be very right and proper that in your special circumstances and in view of accepted public opinion, you should not be called upon to pay your way in respect of this house. But it is none the less necessary that you should understand the position, that you should know where you are in relation to the whole, that you should realise that somebody else is putting forward effort which you, for reasons that we need not go into, are unable to balance. In respect of this particular house, therefore, you are a liability on the community and not an asset to it. It is quite beside the point for you to argue that the money spent on this house was taken from some worthless duke who had more than he was entitled to. That is a subject which may well be argued on its own merits, but it is irrelevant here. You cannot escape the degrading conclusion from your own point of view that you are not paying your way. If you care to go deeper into the matter and contend, as some people do, that the duke has robbed some other poor fellow of the wealth which is now taken from him and put into your house, you will then have to admit that you are benefiting from the robbery of the other poor fellow by the duke and that the other poor fellow really paid for your house, for you cannot in any case maintain that you have done so.

A good deal of interest can be added to life by this interrogatory exercise "Am I paying for it?" When, for instance, I receive a copy of my daily newspaper for twopence, I become possessed of possibly sixpennyworth of paper, print, and editorial effort. And yet I only pay twopence for it. On enquiry I discover that the balance of the cost of all the labour put into my newspaper is paid for me by an advertiser who hopes in that way to secure my custom and develop the market for a brand of petrol or a fountain pen. I can, however, in the case of my newspaper feel perfect comfort in the thought that no one has paid anything towards the cost of my enjoyment unwillingly, by force, or of necessity. Every pennyworth of the whole cost of the newspaper is contributed by those who, in their unfettered judgment, of their perfect freewill, think it wise and proper to maintain this institution of which I am one of the beneficiaries. If my newspaper was provided out of funds collected by force from taxpayers or ratepayers I should have to consider the matter in an entirely different light.

Many people who can honestly say that they are paying their way have to qualify their satisfaction with the knowledge that their work is in the nature of a barren necessity rather than of a benefit to society. For instance, the gentleman in the Ministry of Pensions who enjoys a comfortable home, good clothes and food, an evening now and again at the theatre, and in return spends his time ferreting back twenty years to discover whether the husband of a widow was really a french polisher within the meaning of the Act, and reporting on this important matter so that somebody else may decide whether or not the unfortunate widow is entitled to a pension under the new Act – that man can hardly feel as he surveys his week's effort that he has done very much to provide for the development of the standard of living of the people. There are many in this class, all of them the product of the new politics, all of them quite necessary in the silly sort of society that we have developed out of politics, but none of them by any pretence able to claim that they make their due contribution to the material progress of mankind. The gentleman who stands in a box at Dover or Southampton making smudges on passports, or the skilful and accomplished accountant who brings all the benefits of a higher education to the difficult task of recovering income tax that ought never to have been paid, are doing jobs which must be done, but are both helping to reduce the amount of the product of industry which is available for the rest of us. The worst specimens of this class fill the offices of Whitehall, and spend their time duplicating the work done by corresponding officials of local authorities in obedience to the modern mania for organisation, it being for the moment thought necessary that the council and citizens of Grimsby must not be allowed to lay a drain, build a cottage, or widen a road until a horde of expensive and sophisticated experts in Whitehall have made quite sure that the principles underlying these homely proceedings are in accordance with principles that would also apply to Exeter or Eastbourne.

My suggestion is not that everybody must pay his way. It is merely that everybody should have the matter in mind. When I am knocked down by a taxicab, picked up by a couple of kindly policemen, put into a £1,000 ambulance that costs £20 a week to run, taken to the hospital for free treatment, sent home in the same ambulance, receive free medicine, bandages, and further attendance, draw my health insurance sick pay, and get a new suit of clothes because the owner of the taxicab had the wisdom or was forced by law to insure third parties, who pays for it all? Nobody for one moment will question that I am entitled to all these things so long as society is rich enough to afford them. But it is very important that I, the recipient of wonderful benefits of which my father and my grandfather knew nothing, should be conscious of the fact that they have to be paid for, and give a thought to the ways and means of the matter. This example was brought to my notice through a conversation with a solicitor friend. A young man went through the experience I have described and then, his young mind being crammed full of the modern spirit of grab, consulted his solicitor as to an action for damages against somebody. The lawyer was not unwilling to find a case; it was his business to do so. He did in fact discover a small claim that might be made – for the difference between the sick pay and the wages of the man during his enforced absence from work. As, however, that difference had already been paid by a well-meaning employer, the lawyer, with all his skill, was unable to invent a claim against anybody.

Quite half of us are not expected to pay our way in an economic sense, and no modern society would desire us to do so. There are children, and the aged, and some proportion of the women, but even they ought to know whether they are paying their way or not. Children should surely have some thought

GR

of obligation to their parents put into their little minds. Millions of them in public elementary schools to-day are subjected to lectures on what is strangely called "citizenship," but all too little is said about the realities of their economic life. When we come to the old people, the matter assumes more importance than at any previous time, because medical science is adding so rapidly to the length of life. The Economic Man of the nineteenth century could work out his affairs on a basis of three score years and ten. The Economic Man of the twentieth century is more likely to have to calculate for four score years and ten. His productive period may, perhaps, be rather longer, but the length of his childhood and his unproductive old age will prove to be a larger proportion of his life than was the case with his grandfather.

Women present many interesting problems, but in this connection a quite new one arises, so far little discussed. The Economic Man of the nineteenth century could calculate upon a helpmeet. The recognised function of the woman was to care for the breadwinner, and on this basis many a successful joint career was founded. Now we have to face a new idea. The modern woman must have a career of her own. Man and woman must develop each in his or her own way. Responsibility one to the other is less than it was. Out of this new conception one of two results must emerge. The added economic productivity of the woman may improve the family store of wealth. On the other hand, the more likely result is that neither the man nor the woman will be strong enough to function alone, and the new arrangement will result in a weakening rather than a strengthening of the general economic position.

I am entitled to say that I am paying my way if my money comes from somebody who is free to withhold it, who gives it to me or puts it at my service quite freely and could spend it in some other direction if he so desired. If my father or my husband saved part of his earnings because he thought he would like me to spend them, I am paying my way. If, on the other hand, my money comes from someone who is forced to pay, from rates or taxes for instance, it is as a rule much more difficult for me to be sure that I am giving value, or that any value has been given by anybody, in return.

There are two variations of the question which I have addressed to myself, and which may be mentioned to amplify and strengthen the argument. I might say, "Am I a pauper?" Or, on the other hand, I might usefully ask myself, "How many people am I supporting?" The pauper is "one who through poverty is chargeable to the community," and on that definition there are a great many amongst us who would have to admit ourselves, much as we might dislike the idea, to be paupers. The term "pauper" is out of fashion. We have abolished its use with the destruction of the Boards of Guardians. We talk of "public assistance," or, more generally, "citizens' rights." But paupers in the dictionary sense multiply by millions in obedience to the new theories. All the folk engaged in connection with the manufacture of beet sugar to-day, for instance, are "through poverty chargeable to the community." Their work is of a kind that the rest of the community, in the exercise of their judgment as free buyers, decline to recognise as worth the price demanded. If they had to market their article at a figure which a willing buyer would pay, they would be poverty-stricken, and therefore, as paupers, they charge the balance of their demand to the community. All the owners and workers in derated factories who, by reason of the poverty-stricken condition of industry, are unable to meet their due obligations, would, in any proper classification, be set down as paupers. It is surely a fact that if a public expenditure is a right and proper one, it is the duty of industry to pay for it. All payment has to be made by industry. There is no other source from which any payment can come. To increase public expense to such a point that industry is poverty-stricken, and has to be relieved out of the money which industry alone can provide, is, as Euclid would say, absurd, and yet that is what we are supposed to be doing. The derated factory class must certainly therefore be ranked as paupers. Every man or woman who is taking out of the common till more than he or she puts into it, or more than somebody else puts in with the intention of benefiting that man or woman, is a member of the pauper class, even though the word has disappeared from our vocabulary.

A more cheerful line of enquiry from the real

producer's point of view is opened up by the question, "How many people am I supporting?" The list of those who, while they produce nothing, have to be kept by the producers, grows with every day of the week. The present Government is multiplying them at a rate which will cost the future dear. We must always remember that every non-producer is helping to keep down the real wages of a producer. A civilised society requires for its order and comfort a great many non-producers, but wisdom suggests that the numbers should always be kept as low as circumstances permit. Most people believe that with the world as it is we must have armies, navies, air forces, and police. These all have perforce to share in the product of the rest of the people. But there are others. Members of Parliament at £400 a year; trade union and trade association officials; an enormous professional class engaged entirely in explaining or complying with or devising ways of evading the ever-increasing volume of rule and regulation which the modern politics puts upon us. This class is almost as numerous as the entire body of public officials of all kinds. When, therefore, I ask myself how many people I am supporting, I have to think not only of my family and my natural dependants, but of an ever-increasing proportion of mankind which is finding its occupation in ways that make no contribution to the material wealth of society. My present purpose is not to argue for or against an army, or a Ministry of Health, or a beet sugar factory. I am concerned to reinstate the Economic

Man as we knew him in the nineteenth century. I suggest that if, when discussing our economic "rights," with all the advantages of our modern education, and with the great ability which we have developed for building up our case in the minutest detail, we would take the trouble to add the simple question: Who pays? or, Have I paid? or, Where does the money come from? – we should be more likely to achieve that perfect wisdom which we all desire. If the answer to the question is (as with some of us it certainly will be) that the payment comes from the wealth which a privileged class have robbed from the poor, it does not matter for the purpose of my argument, because such an answer will lead on to the conclusion that when that robbery has ceased, and when that privileged class is exterminated, payment will still have to be made, and some provision must therefore be devised for that contingency. Other people may answer the question in another way. An old age pensioner might reply: "My pension is paid out of super-tax. I enjoy my pension very much. I should like others in time to come to enjoy similar benefits. Therefore I hope that the future will provide an ever-growing and ever-richer number of super-taxpayers, so that there may be more and more pensions for people like me." The nature of the answer to the question is really unimportant. All that is necessary is that it should be asked and an honest endeavour made to answer it.

I conclude this chapter with a paragraph which, by all the ordinary rules of journalism, should have appeared in the *Daily Herald*. That paper was good enough to ask me to make a short contribution to a symposium on "The Perfect Income." On further consideration, however, the editor thought, or so I flatter myself, that my definition of a perfect income had more wisdom in it than would appeal to his readers. This is what I said:

"The perfect income is that which, as it goes into the pocket, brings into the heart and mind a sense of satisfaction and justice. The man who, when he gets his money, whatever it is, can feel that he has given value in return, enjoys a perfect satisfaction which is denied to all the rest. Whatever the system under which we live may be called, the fact remains that we have to render service to one another, and to exchange those services each with the others. We should all put something into the commonwealth and all take something out of it. If when we count up our incomes, be they large or small, we have a feeling that they are something less than the contribution which we have made to the common well-being, we can claim that our incomes reach as near to perfection as is possible in a work-a-day world."

CHAPTER VIII

THE NATURAL GROWTH OF EXPENDITURE

NOTHING is easier than to criticise the details of an account, especially an account of public expenditure. Criticism generally takes the form of alternative ways of spending the money. We all feel aggrieved that economy should be practised in connection with some work which interests us, and each of us is inclined to be unsympathetic towards expenditure on other work which we do not understand. This is one of those difficulties for which there is no remedy, as our private conversation shows. One woman will think that her neighbour should spend less on her clothes and more on her kitchen, and a man will fail to understand why some friend should put half a crown a week into tobacco and be blind to the wisdom of adequate life insurance. There are, however, natural differences in the character of private and public expenditure, and weighty reasons why these differences should be studied and remembered. Private expenditure is always subject to the limitation of private resources, while public expenditure appears to know no such limitation. The war killed the last remnants of the Victorian sense of care and economy in public finance. There were financiers of repute in the autumn of 1914 who satisfied themselves that the war must end by the following Christmas because no more money would be

available. Those people have since learnt that public
expenditure can be supported on the abstract
theory of public credit in a way which is entirely
denied to private expenditure. The public can
abuse the machinery of finance in such a way as to
put the burden upon posterity. Private finance, on
the other hand, is limited in its ability to be foolish
by the amount of the savings of the past. It is to
distinctions such as these that we must attribute
the rapid progress of public expenditure in the last
few years, and in these respects the analogy between family finance and national finance ceases
to be good. A search through the public accounts
of recent years fails to disclose any department,
large or small, to which the principles of economy,
as understood in family finance, have to any appre-
ciable extent been applied. Every figure grows and
goes on growing, and, further, as I shall submit, is
from its nature bound to grow until we begin to
look at these matters in an entirely different way.

Take the cost of the collection of the revenue
itself. In 1917–18 the branch of the Civil Service
which is typified to us by Somerset House cost
£3,195,155, or 0.6 per cent. of the revenue collected.
In 1928–29 the cost of collection of the inland
revenue was £7,782,580, or 1.7 per cent. of the
revenue. Here is an increase of four and a half
millions, representing less than two days' revenue
out of the three hundred and sixty-five, and almost
a detail to a people who have learnt to think in
thousands of millions. But, when examined, it
brings out very clearly this natural, inherent, and,

as I think, irremovable tendency of all public expenditure to increase. It will be noticed that every pound collected into the public purse cost in 1928–29 nearly three times as much to get as a pound did in 1917–18. The clerks in a commercial office will be fully conscious all the time of the necessity for keeping the costs of the counting-house within a given percentage of the revenue of the business. They know that the accounts of the business must balance, that the gross product of the sales is the total of the sum to be divided between them and many others. They have in their minds the necessity for economy, for expedition, for the cutting out of useless processes, and generally for the promotion of efficiency. They know that these are the only ways in which their own personal prospects can be bettered. A counting-house, therefore, in a commercial undertaking, will tend to cost an ever lower percentage of the gross receipts while providing an ever better personal return to the clerks who work in it. But the clerk in the inland revenue office, from the very nature of things, is denied the advantages of this point of view. The higher officials may be, and generally are, anxious to keep the costs of their departments low, but their power to resist the ever-growing demands for higher pay is not subject to the limitations of the commercial world, and they cannot point to the balance-sheet and say, " There is no more to be got." The point is seen very clearly when we turn to an institution like the Ministry of Agriculture. There is no other

excuse in the whole realm of reason for most of the
operations of this swollen concern than the
natural ambition of a bureaucracy to promote its
own personal interests. In 1913-14 we satisfied
our desire to control and regulate agriculture with
the modest sum of £264,312. That was the total
of the Budget figure for the whole of the agricultural
department in the year before the war. In 1929-
30 the Ministry of Agriculture is spending
£2,953,863. The bill has gone up eleven times, and
heads the list of proportionate increases. The
bureaucrats who have chosen agriculture as the
subject of their attentions have outstripped all
their fellows in the race for expansion and expense.
They have, no doubt, benefited to a large extent
from the weakness or the cleverness of politicians,
who always find it easy to appear wise about
agriculture when appealing for the suffrages of an
urban electorate.

It remains for Whitehall to justify the exploits
of its most successful men and women, who have
put all the other departments to shame in the
race for squandering public funds. Agriculture, if
we are to believe what is said about it by the very
few vocal agriculturists, is in a sorry way – indeed,
has never been so badly hit. If in our private
affairs, after fifteen years, our expenditure had
been multiplied by eleven in vain pursuance of a
particular policy, and our trade had gone from
bad to worse, no one would hesitate to alter that
policy. The case is clear that the expenditure of
all this money and the interference which it

represents have so damaged agriculture as to call
for an immediate change. It is hard to imagine
any branch of human activity in which official
assistance can be of less service. All the agricultural shows, the gardening societies, the local
competitions and displays, are tending to weaken
because of the time which our farmers have to
waste in filling up official forms and receiving
with due respect the many inspectors and instruc-
tors who are foisted upon them.

Education is in another category. It is not only
an industrial or an economic problem. There is a
healthy unanimity of opinion that education
should be fostered, and no advocate of economy
could hope to win much favour if he devoted too
much of his criticism to expenditure on education.
Nevertheless, the figures must be studied, and
they provide an admirable illustration of the way
in which the public purse is without any of the
healthy safeguards of the private purse. In 1913–14
the average attendance of children in the elementary schools was 5,381,479. The cost was
£30,011,000. To-day the average attendance in
elementary schools is 4,890,000, or 10 per cent.
less than fifteen years ago. The cost, however, is
£79,660,000, or 163 per cent. more. While some of
this money has gone to the proper purposes of
education, most of it has been squandered on the
administrative side of the great machine which
cannot resist the tendency for more forms, more
returns, more complications, more expense.

The figures for other social services grow because

of new demands, and it is not possible to be sure how much is due to the satisfaction of those demands and how much to inherent administrative extravagance. In 1891 social services cost us £22,644,000; in 1911, £68,158,000; and in 1927, £383,261,000. The people as a whole must share with the bureaucracy the responsibility for any evil there may be in this total. It is perhaps the most striking of the fruits of victory. Having suffered in life and treasure unparalleled losses in a great war, having wiped out almost all that was worth having in a whole generation, we in our folly thought it well to embark upon an orgy of extravagance in the name of social service, and to lead all our people to believe that we were better off than before. Any blame that may attach to this extraordinary course must be shouldered by the nation as a whole.

One general conclusion can be drawn from these few examples of the growth of national expenditure. That growth is natural and inevitable if we accept the policy which governs these matters to-day. Public expenditure being from its nature unable to benefit from the safeguards that belong to every other form of expenditure, it must tend to grow. We have, if we care to take advantage of it, the example of Australia to indicate to us what is likely to happen unless we do reverse our policy. Australia has had far more experience of social legislation than the mother country. She has for long been the pride of the advocates of a progressive labour and legislative policy, and years ago

boasted that next to America she had the highest
standard of living in the world. She was in this
sort of condition in 1919, with a public debt of
£325,000,000 and an annual expenditure of
£45,000,000. Since then she has proceeded apace
to develop further all those services and benefits
with which we are now experimenting. Above all,
she has brought to perfection the theory of cen-
tralisation, and in the development of the united
Commonwealth has secured uniformity of administration and all the theoretical economies which
come from the rationalisation of public work and
services. What has been the result? Ten years
later, in 1929, the public debt was £541,986,000,
and the annual expenditure £81,343,000. In the
end, Australia is driven to such drastic measures
as the prohibition of imports, which does not, after
all, matter very much, seeing that, as she is quite
unable to pay, nobody is likely to do very much
exporting to her. I imagine that a full examina-
nation of the course of events in Australia in the
last ten years would cause us anxiously and
rapidly to set about undoing most of the things
we have done in Parliament and Whitehall since
we came under the influence of the new politics.

Our Civil Service is the finest institution of the
kind in the world, a fact which does not surprise
us, or those of us who still believe that the Englishman in most departments of human affairs knows
how to do things rather better than other less
favoured people. But because our Civil Service is
the finest in the world, because most of our Civil

Servants are actuated by the highest motives, because we are free from graft and other similar abuses, we are not relieved from the necessity of studying the nature of a Civil Service and its fundamental inability, however perfectly it may be worked, to undertake particular classes of function. The most obvious thing about a Civil Servant is that no natural method or means exist for testing his quality, his ability, or his fitness for the service he is supposed to render. It is not our habit to tell a friend or an acquaintance that he is an incompetent fool. We leave him to find it out. If he is in business he will in time discover it, not because someone will inform him of the fact in so many words, but because bit by bit his trade and his income will leave him. The Civil Servant is altogether free from the operations of any such healthy process. His customers cannot leave him. They have to queue up outside his office for a birth certificate, a motor licence, a postage stamp, or even to pay their income tax. They have no option in the matter. It is not possible for a Civil Service customer to say : " The registrar of births and deaths at Brighton does the job rather better than the one at Southampton, and therefore I will patronise Brighton." The unfortunate customer who finds himself under the necessity of registering the death of his wife may have to walk three miles to the appointed office, only to find that the service does not work until eleven o'clock on the following morning and he must come back again. The same principle applies right through.

These people render what is so strangely called service with the bludgeon of an Act of Parliament in one hand and a pen in the other, and the unfortunate served has no opportunity at any stage of any of the proceedings to express an opinion about it. That again is in the nature of things and there is no remedy, but it is worth noting in passing that it also robs the Civil Servant of the stimulating advantages of competition or of test of quality of any sort, kind, or description.

All this is not to say that as many good, active, energetic men are not to be found in the Civil Service as in the ranks of business itself. The Englishman is an active creature. He wants to get on personally even though he may be denied the competitive idea in theory. But the man in business who would get on must do so by attracting more and more customers to himself. He must therefore offer more and more advantages, and the worth of the advantages will always be tested by the willingness of free customers to avail themselves of them. The Civil Servant who wants to get on goes to work in a very different way. He cannot attract more and more customers. He must strive to bring more and more people under the lash of authority. They may be mere ratepayers outside the building or clerks inside. Both serve the same purpose. In the Ministry of Munitions, where I had the privilege of masquerading as a Civil Servant for a time, we were all working away anxiously and vigorously to win the war, but few of us were able to shake off entirely those little

personal considerations which do after all count
with most people. My little section was certainly
influenced by the fact that an office which could
boast of seventy-five clerks had a superior status.
The principal shorthand typist became a *secretary*-
shorthand typist, received a slightly higher wage,
was entitled to work at a double pedestal desk, to
have a mirror as well as a typewriter, and a piece
of indiarubber. The head of such a section could,
by the rules of the department, claim first-class
fares when travelling. The official who could
contrive to develop a number of such sections under
his direction would in due course appear upon the
list to be submitted to the Minister for the quota
of honours which twice a year was allotted to the
Ministry. Thus in many little ways the natural
urge to importance promoted extravagance, and
it is difficult to criticise the very proper desire of
the meanest of us to add another ribbon or stripe
or pair of stockings to our social equipment. These
forces are at work all the time.

In the public service everything must be checked
and re-checked, examined and re-examined, and
criticised from every conceivable point of view. A
man who is acting in the name of the public must
be ready to meet every objection that can be raised
to his actions and to justify every dot and comma
in his documents, not by the test of common sense
and expediency, but by the technical interpretation
of a single word or phrase. This sort of thing is
going on all the time. It involves more and more
staff in every labour exchange in the country, and

Hr

is essential to the working of the present system.

In the Ministry of Munitions, whether I was actuated by a desire to win the war, or wished to do my job well, or hoped to add to the importance of my department, does not matter. I acted within my undoubted rights and indented every other department in the Ministry so that I might receive their papers and memoranda, and thus know what they were doing and be able to frame my proceedings in accordance with theirs. Government departments must act upon uniform principles. It is true that by this device and in pursuance of this obviously necessary policy I succeeded in getting my fingers into a number of other pies. I may have been successful here and there in arresting imprudent activity, but I undoubtedly caused many and serious delays in connection with other matters which would have made more progress without my interference. I was, however, both the beneficiary and the victim of the system.

It is surprising to think that in a practical world we have got ourselves into such an unpractical way of thinking that we attach an importance to all the tomfoolery of official procedure which is denied to the operations of private work and effort. If some silly paper can be labelled "official," it takes precedence in the Post Office, and even in our own correspondence, over a private document, even though the latter may be of great practical importance and urgency. A recent personal experience illustrates this absurd state of affairs. The roadway in Fleet Street, one of the busiest streets in the world, required repairs. A gang of men was employed on the work, and performed it in accordance with the rules and regulations of their trade. At lunch-time they picnicked, sitting round the sides of a hole eating bread and cheese and drinking tea. The traffic from east and west was regulated by two extra policemen, and was in a solid block from Cannon Street on the one side to Charing Cross on the other. The thousands of newspaper workers who swarmed the street in the middle of the day threaded their difficult way through the obstruction, and the whole of this centre of one of our most important industries was blocked, hindered, and delayed while eight or nine men boiled tea and ate bread and cheese. The same evening I happened to be in Whitehall. There is a little street on the Charing Cross side of the War Office which leads nowhere in particular and which is very little used. I myself have frequently used it as a promenade when I wanted a quiet chat with a friend. I know of no street in the whole of London where there is less traffic, either vehicular or pedestrian. But at nine o'clock that night the flares were at work, the automatic drills active, and gangs of men were busy repairing that comparatively useless little thoroughfare. The difference between a street bordering upon the War Office, even though nobody uses it, and Fleet Street, the centre of the Press of the world, is that the one is in the official area and the other is concerned merely with private enterprise. Some brass hat, organising a staff of clerks which is twice as big per soldier as before the war may, I suspect, have written a note to the Town Clerk of Westminster to call attention to the difficulties of conducting official work while road repairs are in progress. In obedience to some such absurd pretension, ratepayers will be charged with overtime, trade unions will relax their rules, and every other consideration will stand aside. If, however, instead of a question of State like the width of the braid on the trousers of a second-lieutenant, the problem is the getting of a London newspaper to Euston in time to catch the northern mails, the road repairer declines to be interested, and goes on boiling his tea in the middle of Fleet Street at the busiest time of the day. It may be difficult for those who have never considered these matters to understand their full import. I remember how, when I was wasting the money of the nation doing all sorts of silly things under the guidance of Dr. Addison at the Ministry of Reconstruction, I could get a telephone fixed in Queen Anne's Gate within a few hours at any time of the day or night, and I remember how, returning to the City and resuming my unofficial character, I spent weeks in an endeavour to secure a telephone installation for my offices.

Work in the Civil Service, however necessary, always tends to assume an artificial character, is always a matter of form rather than substance, and yet is still regarded by common consent as of more importance, more urgency, and deserving of more consideration, than work which has for its object the supply of some necessary, practical, human need.

In examining the Account Rendered for the Civil Service, and in going over the figures of all these departments, we have to take into account very much more than an odd million sovereigns here and there, and endeavour to understand the purport, the meaning, and the usefulnesss, of all this Government business. If the ideas of the last twenty-five years are right and proper, then we are doomed, whether we like it or not, and in spite of all the economy campaigns, to an ever growing bureaucracy and to an ever greater expense. It will not, in a way, be the fault of Parliament, although of course Parliament is nominally responsible. The charge must be laid against the lazy, unthinking public mind, which declines to study the practical effects of many of the things which it permits to be done. Public extravagance and private extravagance have this in common – that they both arise from a lack of grip upon realities – and the cure for both is a recultivation of that practical sense of economy and values which characterised the last century.

"There is another sort of aristocracy which is forming, growing, increasing daily in numbers and power, of which one does not often think and at whose existence Tocqueville hinted: it is bureaucracy. . . . The Civil Service in France, and in most of the European countries, is actually an almost autonomous body, and one which will be rendered more and more autonomous by democratic customs. It is not elected, it recruits itself; it is even somewhat hereditary, in the sense that it is always drawn from the same social class, the middle class; it has traditions, habits, special customs, *esprit de corps*, a certain general spirit which is unchanging; it has fairly strong professional qualities, much esteem for itself, its appearance, and its dignity; it holds the secret of the management of affairs and cannot be dispensed with. . . . It increases incessantly in numbers and importance, because, in centralised societies, everything tends to become governmental, and anything which becomes governmental comes within the province of the Civil Service. It is the modern aristocracy. In truth its autonomy is in no way constitutional and legal. It is only a collection of agents in the hands of the central authority. But democracy, by strengthening the central authority and making it more variable, merely strengthens the Civil Service which it does not appoint. . . . This aristocracy will surely be maintained for a very long time and, like parliaments formerly, will be strong under weak Governments, reserved and timid under accidentally strong Governments, until the day when democracy will feel that an aristocracy – that is to say, an independent power – has arisen, and will demand that Government officials be elected."[1]

[1] Émile Faguet: *Politicians and Moralists of the Nineteenth Century.*

CHAPTER IX

FASHIONS IN GOVERNMENT

OUR study of the Account Rendered will be imperfect if it is limited to the consideration of figures. The owners of a gold-mine deceive themselves if in reckoning the output of the metal they forget that the seam is coming to an end, or, conversely, that another seam has been discovered. Equally, in studying the national accounts we should remember that nine-tenths of our machinery of government was unknown so recently as thirty years ago, and, please God, most of it will be forgotten thirty years hence. A law which prohibits the reporting of divorce proceedings and doubles the number of divorces, all within a period of two or three years, is not in the same class as the laws of the Medes and Persians, and most of our modern laws are of this order.

Of all the various and confused aims, ambitions, desires, and passions, which make life worth living, the wish to govern takes a high and honourable place. To steer, to pilot, or to direct the affairs of the society in which he lives is the proper aim of the good citizen who desires to see his social ideals put into effect. But this urge to govern differs in at least one important respect from other urges that bless or afflict the human being, inasmuch as it is concerned wholly with the affairs of others. Doubtless whatever we do in pursuance of any of

our desires, good or bad, has some influence on the
happiness of *some* others, but when we indulge our
ambitions in the way of government we necessarily
exercise an influence, good or bad, on the affairs
of *all* others. We can, for instance, hold and express sincere opinions on some point in theology
without the risk of ordering the thoughts and lives
of others, for theology is by general consent outside the proper limits of the business of government, and our desire to influence others must be
exercised through persuasion and not by force. We
may threaten penalities in the next world, but must
leave complete liberty in this one. If, on the other
hand, we hold and express opinions on the raising
of the school age, education being within the accepted limits of government, we shoulder the tre-
mendous responsibility of exercising a vital influence upon the actions and lives of all our fellows.
And while we recognise that life itself is not long
enough to understand and master the many-sided
problems of theology, we carelessly accept twenty-
one years and a vote as proof of perfect wisdom on
the proportion of life which shall perforce be spent
in pursuit of a statutory system of exercises which
we dignify with the title of education. "We are
none of us content," Herbert Spencer told us,
"with quietly unfolding our own individualities;
but have a restless craving to impress our individualities on others, and in some way to subordin-
ate them," a state of affairs which is tolerable only
if the others are always free to escape the subor-
dination, and wholly dangerous when the impress

is performed in the name of authority and all are subordinated by force.

Interference is, of course, the essence of government. Most governments at one time have indulged in various forms of interference with religious views and practices and at another have turned their interfering powers towards the economic activities of their peoples. It has remained for the new Russian Government to attempt the bigger task of regulating both the material and the ethical in one wholesale system which claims to order both the thoughts and actions of all its subjects.

Government is the last of the shams of civilisation. In what is thought to be a perfect democracy I govern by right, but whatever else I want to do must be accomplished by work and endeavour. If I am twenty-one years of age I cast my vote for seven hours for a miner, the abolition of the submarine, the increase of the National Debt, the taxation of company reserves, or Dominion status for India, without any questions asked as to my qualifications. When, however, I desire to work as a compositor I must serve a seven years' apprenticeship. The minor things, the practical details, the commonplace necessities of life are recognised to be difficult, but the big things, issues of universal import, world affairs, the regulation of life and happiness, depend upon a right which all are supposed to possess and expected to exercise. Strangely enough, this is a subject which is hardly discussed. Somebody proposes, let us say, that the price of wheat should be fixed at a certain figure, and that extremely technical and difficult proposition is submitted almost automatically to thirty million electors and to as many newspaper readers. The discussion will be loud and vigorous for and against the proposed price, for and against the method of fixing, for and against the principle involved, but nobody will deny the right to act, or still less the qualifications of the thirty million electors to discuss the matter at all. There was a time when men were burnt for holding doctrines in conflict with the teaching of the dominant Church, and there is no technical reason to prevent our thirty million electors re-enacting some such salutary penalty for some such offence. But meanwhile we have shelved the difficulties and inconveniences of the faggot and the stake by the development of a public opinion that bans the powers and processes of government from the religious field. We have, however, while relieving a few individuals here and there of the sacrifice of martyrdom, transferred the powers and processes of government to the filling or the emptying of every stomach in the race.

The time will no doubt come when the folly of government action in the matter of wheat and other commodities will be as apparent as it now is in the case of theological doctrine, and then economic progress will be as free and rapid as religious development. There was a time when the man who suggested that governments could do no good in religious matters would have been

regarded as impiously lacking in understanding of
the principles of good government. It is similarly
going well beyond public opinion to-day to suggest
that in matters of economics government is outside its proper sphere. Nevertheless, a day may
come when interference with the people's food or
houses will be tolerated no more than interference
with their religious beliefs.

The fact is that since the days of Machiavelli we
have never applied ourselves to the study of
government as an abstract subject. This generation turns to government as its grandfathers
turned to God, and looks upon it as an ever-
present help in trouble. Some of us believe in the
efficacy of prayer, but a great many more believe
in the power of government to fix a wage, to find
us work, or to save us from our own incapacities.
Here, apparently, is no matter for argument; we
are under the arbitrary dictates of fashion in
opinion. Fashion is a despotic jade; she changes her
mind and imposes new ideas with equally un-
reasoning force. If, however, democracy is made of
no better stuff than to serve fashion's fancy, the
sooner we get rid of democracy the better for
civilisation. I am one of those who think that there
is sterner stuff in democracy, and that its quality
will before long begin to make itself apparent.
Critics of the present state of affairs are apt to take
short views and thus arrive at wrong conclusions.
We English have been at this government business
in a steady conscious way for ten centuries, having
all that time no other object than to transfer the

powers of government from various sorts of despots into the hands of the people themselves. Even ten centuries have not given us time enough to enquire as to the *nature* of government; we have been far too busy arguing that it was in the wrong hands. And now no sincere democrat will venture to doubt that government is in the right hands; the people are really governing themselves. To quite half the people the experience is a novel one and the quality of government is therefore very poor. There are thirty million electors playing with government in much the same way as the school-boy plays with a new watch. In the course of time the boy will learn that the less the attention he gives to the watch the better will be its time-keeping qualities, and equally it is no vain hope that even thirty million electors will one day discover that the quality of government improves as the quantity diminishes.

The necessity for a study of the possibilities and limitations of the thing called government is obvious to anyone who will note the conversation of a single day and count the number of suggestions made by his friends in that short period. Within the last twenty-four hours good, sensible, well-meaning people have expressed the restless craving to impress their individualities on others by asking me to agree with them that the Government should: (1) Buy all the wheat supplies; (2) Stop motor-cycle trials; (3) Prohibit the wearing of hats; (4) Stop the sale of alcoholic drink; (5) Keep all the children; (6) Allow no horses on the roads

after 8 a.m.; (7) Abolish the Navy; (8) Double the
Air Force; (9) Fix the bank rate; (10) Censor books;
and (11) License prostitution: these sundry little
matters being in addition to the more popular
proposals common to the political parties, such
as uniting the Empire, abolishing poverty, and
finding employment for all. But, strangely enough,
nobody in this one day's talk has touched on the
question of government itself. Not one of these
reformers has doubted for a moment that his
proposal was within the proper powers and functions of government. Mr. and Mrs. Sidney Webb
have written a great deal about the machinery of
government, and indeed may claim great credit for
having designed a modern automatic monster
whose wheels revolve with clockwork precision, as
soulless as a rotary press, as foolproof as a penny-
in-the-slot machine, and equipped with mechanical
suckers which draw every citizen, from infancy to
old age, into its clutches. But not a single line or
sentence in the whole Webb library ever hints that
there may perchance be odd things which the
Government cannot wisely undertake, or things
which might be better done by other agencies.

A study of the subject is the more worth while at
the present moment, when the democratic system,
of which we are the special guardians, is beginning
to be questioned in every part of the world. The
principal of democracy is threatened because of
the folly displayed in its application. If we really
persist in thinking that government means building houses, filling stomachs or even paying wages,

and if democratic government involves the permanent acceptance of these destructive fallacies, then the nations which are giving up the theory that they can govern themselves are those that will eventually govern the rest of us. We badly need a second Hobbes who, having determined the origin of sovereignty, will discuss for us the limits of its application for good. Three hundred years ago we learnt from his *Leviathan* that "amongst men, there are very many that think themselves wiser and abler to govern the Publique, better than the rest; and these strive to reform and innovate, one this way, another that way; and thereby bring it into Distraction and Civil War."

We of the twentieth century enjoy many advantages from the reforms and innovations of the past, but a new Hobbes would probably tell us that those advantages have always been of an ethical, social, or political character, and that no permanent or useful economic advance can be attributed to those who "think themselves wiser and abler to govern." Instead of doing good in the economic sphere it may transpire that the dabbling of Government in matters outside its true province has only robbed us of the benefits of Government in its higher moral applications. "The worth of a state, in the long run, is the worth of the individuals composing it; and a state which postpones the interests of *their* mental expansion and elevation, to a little more of administrative skill, or of that semblance of it which practice gives, in the details of business; a state which dwarfs its men, in order that they may be more docile instruments in its hands even for beneficial purposes, will find that with small men no great thing can really be accomplished; and that the perfection of machinery to which it has sacrificed everything, will in the end avail it nothing, for want of the vital power which, in order that the machine might work more smoothly, it has preferred to banish."[1]

[1] John Stuart Mill: *On Liberty*.

CHAPTER X

A SAMPLE OF MODERN LEGISLATION

MUCH of the legislation resulting from the new politics would fail to get beyond a first reading if the electors could be persuaded to take only so much interest in these matters as to read for themselves the Bills which now find their way with devastating rapidity into the pages of the Statute Book. Lord Hewart, in *The New Despotism*, has given it as his opinion – and no man speaks with more authority – that our modern laws originate with the new bureaucracy and that many of them have no other excuse for existence than the natural desire of our bureaucrats for power and aggrandisement. We are supposed to govern ourselves, but when put to the test the supposition proves to be a very slender one. In practice some State department looking for work notices, say, discontent among the farmers; the politicians looking for popularity proclaim that "something must be done." In the end the politician gets the credit and the bureaucrat gets the salary for doing something which we do not bother to understand, are too careless to enquire about, and which as often as not produces results of an opposite character to those for which we thought we voted. The ordinary self-governing citizen takes no interest in his laws until a policeman or a solicitor informs him that he shall not do something he badly wants to do, and then he writes to the newspapers to suggest further laws which, when enacted, generally make his position still more impossible.

I have printed as an Appendix the Agricultural Marketing Bill, 1930. I would prefer to print it as my first chapter, for I regard a full and careful study of its every phrase as the bounden duty of any reader who would really understand the position in which we find ourselves and the reasons why trade and industry fail to function smoothly. The reader possessed of any business experience will, on perusing this typical Parliamentary Bill, have no shadow of doubt in his mind that from the day it passes into law agriculture will go steadily from bad to worse. A study of this market-killing instrument, and the reflection that a hundred similar stupidities have been imposed upon the coal-mines, may enable some readers to solve for themselves a few of the problems which trouble the unfortunate mining industry. For my part, I do not doubt that if our bureaucrats succeed in getting as firm a hold on agriculture as they have on mines, we shall speedily experience as much trouble and expense in securing an egg or a potato as we now do with our necessary coals. I select for my present purpose the Agricultural Marketing Bill because it happens to be on my desk as I write, but there are several other measures at present before Parliament, or likely soon to be discussed, any of which would serve equally well. The Factories Bill, the Consumers' Council Bill, the promised Catering Trade Board, and the further

IR

Town Planning Bill to follow the new Housing Act, are each full of prospective unemployment, and each threatens our standard of work and living.

The Agricultural Marketing Bill is recommended to the electors on the simple grounds that co-operation among farmers would be helpful to farming. It does not occur to those who support the measure that farmers themselves may be the best judges of the possibilities of co-operation, nor do they bother to notice that a very great deal of practical co-operation already exists. But the ostensible purpose of the measure should be remembered as the Bill is read, because it is hard to find much about it in the phraseology of the Bill itself. The plan is apparently that if and when the farmers of an area decide to co-operate, or, failing that, when the Minister decides that they must co-operate, there shall immediately swoop down upon them a horde of officials who will then become the masters of the situation.

Leaving contentious questions aside for the moment, there are some results which all will agree must follow immediately upon the passing of this measure. First and most obvious, the "aggregate expenses" of the Ministry of Agriculture are "not expected to exceed £20,000 per annum." This modest amount will therefore be added to the bureaucrats' wage-fund, and at first sight and in these days looks so paltry as to be unworthy of comment. The next generation, gifted with a greater sense of economy, may not regard with such equanimity an obligation to maintain an expensive staff with claims for promotion and rights to pensions in respect of work which should never be performed. If, in contradiction of all experience, this £20,000 is an adequate estimate, the Treasury will disburse at least £500,000 before it has completely discharged all the obligations to this new bunch of bureaucrats assumed on the day when they are appointed.

The £20,000, with an ultimate half a million, represents, however, only the "aggregate expenses incurred by the Minister" out of "moneys provided by Parliament." £625,000 more is to be provided by Parliament, at once, "for the purpose of financing boards administering the schemes," and if any critic should venture to question our ability to find this money he will no doubt be told from the front bench that the money will be reproductive and is really only wanted for banking purposes. The fact that Chancellors can raid funds when successful, as in the case of roads, or that other funds, when bankrupt, as Unemployment Insurance, have to be supported by further grants, and that, generally speaking, no funds with which Parliament parts ever get back to the taxpayers' pockets, is not the sort of criticism which the present sort of Parliament shows any inclination to consider.

Passing from these simple considerations, and having, as it were, the money in hand, the Bill with characteristic care sets out a number of the duties which the Minister is to perform. He shall, for instance, "cause an account to be prepared and transmitted to the Comptroller and Auditor-General for examination on or before the thirtieth day of September in every year," etc. But no mention is made of the necessary expenses of the Comptroller and Auditor-General in receiving and examining and reporting upon such accounts. The fact that the activities of one department increase the expenses of another, and that neither is responsible for this automatic rise in the tax-payer's burden is still another of those small points of criticism for which current fashions of thought leave no room. This Bill invokes the aid of the Companies Act, 1929, Part x.; sub-section 2 of section thirty-eight of the Interpretation Act, 1889; the *London Gazette*; the *Edinburgh Gazette*; the Industrial and Provident Societies Acts, 1893 to 1928 (except that paragraph (*a*) of the proviso to section four of that Act shall in its application to such society have effect as if five hundred pounds were substituted for two hundred pounds); the Agricultural Credits Scotland Act, 1929; the High Court; the Court of Session; the Treasury; the Board of Trade; the Secretary of State for Scotland; section one hundred and twenty-six of the County Courts Act, 1888; the Bills of Sale Acts, 1878 and 1882; and Part II. of the Agricultural Credits Act, 1928. Seeing that the offices and persons charged with the administration of all these matters will, by reason of the new Act, have new duties and extra work put upon them, and seeing further that many other Government departments will promptly and

properly find an interest in the workings of the
new measure, the "aggregate" expenses of the Minister of Agriculture so modestly put at £20,000 become almost an incident beside the expenses of the
extra clerks and extra offices added to other State
departments by this Act. In this matter this
measure is no exception to the general rule whereby every Act adds to the expenses of every department and all expenses are forced to grow while no
responsibility for the growth can be placed upon
anybody. If therefore we double the Minister's
£20,000, and with the permanent employment and
pension rights associated with the Civil Service we
put the ultimate liability at a million sterling, we
cannot be accused of over-estimating the new
obligations to be met "out of moneys provided by
Parliament."

Passing on to what may be described as our subsidiary bureaucracy, it will be noticed that the Bill
inflicts upon us, if it becomes generally operative,
a whole new class of inspectors and annoyers the
cost of which is not, because it cannot be, specified,
but which will again multiply our £20,000 many
times over. Every district or area is to have (1) An
Agricultural Marketing Board, (2) a Consumers'
Committee, and (3) a Committee of Investigation;
and these three bodies in every locality, each with
the approval of the other two, are to embark upon
a comprehensive scheme for regulating the life of
every pig, chicken, and carrot in the land from the
cradle to the grave. They are to have powers to
"enter and inspect, at any reasonable time, any

land or premises occupied by a registered producer, and to inspect and take copies of any books, accounts, or other documents kept by him, relating to the regulated product." They are to prescribe the forms in which producers are to keep "estimates, returns, accounts, and other information," so that amongst other things they may furnish returns to the Minister of milk, potatoes, hops, wool, cereals, cheese, and livestock, and thus provide Whitehall with the work it so generously undertakes to perform for a sum provided by Parliament and not expected to exceed £20,000 per annum.

Before therefore we proceed to consider the wisdom or otherwise of all this machinery, and its probable effect upon the supply and the price of agricultural produce, it is well to notice that the Bill makes an addition to the general public expenses of another army of subsidiary bureaucrats. These will always tend to multiply as the complications of control develop, and their multiplication will involve corresponding increases in the number and importance of the workers in Whitehall.

Coming from the bureaucrats and subsidiary bureaucrats to the mere farmers and workers who, after all, are the people who provide our food, it will be agreed that a great many new intellectual interests are added to their practical obligations. To begin with, nobody may henceforth sell an egg or a potato who is neither "a registered producer or a person exempted from registration by or under the provisions of the scheme." So that applications on prescribed forms either for registration or for exemption must be considered by three committees before anybody can set a hen to work in a backyard of an area within the range of a scheme. Whether or not the Comptroller and Auditor-General will report to Parliament on or before the thirtieth of September in every year on the growth of unemployment among hens as a result of this little bit of official discouragement does not appear from the phraseology of the Act.

The kind, variety, grade, quantity, price, and everything about every agricultural product is to be the subject of regulation in such a way as to satisfy both producers and consumers. Could anything be more absurd ?

The manner in which every duckling or pint of milk is to be "graded, packed, stored, adapted for sale, insured, advertised, or transported" is to be subject to the approval of three committees working through their numerous officers. "The persons to, or through the agency of, whom the product or any kind, variety, grade or quantity thereof may be sold" are to be determined by the same committees – and so on. Those who have studied *The New Despotism* will not be surprised to find that in its seventeen pages of absurd elaboration on the duties and functions of boards and committees and officials, the Act really settles nothing and merely places in the hands of the Minister of Agriculture new power to do anything he likes in any of these matters. "The

Minister, if he thinks fit so to do . . . may by order make such amendments in the scheme as he considers necessary or expedient . . . may by order revoke the scheme . . . and in particular may . . . provide that the board shall . . . be composed wholly or partly of persons nominated by the Minister." So that in future any farmer wishing to sow a field of oats, when his local committee prefers barley, will miss the season while Whitehall considers the matter. All of which is solemnly to be enacted by "the King's most Excellent Majesty, by and with the advice and consent of the Lords Spiritual and Temporal, and Commons, in this present Parliament assembled."

I beg the reader to resist any inclination to rely upon this brief comment, and to give himself the trouble of reading the full text of the Bill as printed in the Appendix. Having done so, I further ask that the reader will remember that this is only one of hundreds of similar enactments, and that many of them affect other trades and occupations in much the same way. A study, for instance, of the numerous building Acts will disclose vexations put upon builders, many of them no more reasonable than the proposed handicaps for agriculture, and, as some may think, more than sufficient to explain any troubles or inconveniences we may suffer from inadequate housing accommodation. Freedom, no doubt, has its disadvantages, but regulation in the modern manner makes any form of activity well-nigh impossible and forces unemployment upon us.

The only sensible line in this monstrous but typical Bill and the only line which does not involve the taxpayer in expense is Clause 18, section 2.

CHAPTER XI

GODSTONE AS AN EXAMPLE

Good auditors examine accounts from several different points of view. They will not only report upon the general position of an undertaking, but will check up the figures of some of the smaller departments. They will sometimes find that, while the account as a whole is bad, there are saving features in the details from which a more favourable impression can be gained.

In considering our position as a nation in the year 1930 and following this plan, it would be easy to produce details of a very disquieting nature. We could set out the accounts of Poplar, Chester-le-Street, or West Ham and draw conclusions from those places which would be false if applied to other more fortunate areas. But having discovered so much to cause us anxiety in the account as a whole, it would serve us better to search about for bright spots, little corners where we may expect to find, if not perfect economy, at least substantial solvency.

We have to admit that after a very difficult period, with its war and other troubles, certain industrial areas are bound to disclose in their accounts weaknesses which would not exist in more normal times. Therefore in our search for a ray of hope and encouragement it would be better to seek out a locality which may happily have escaped some if not all of these unusual complications.

The Rural District of Godstone is one of the most favoured spots in delightful Surrey. Although it lies within twenty miles of London it is almost entirely unspoilt, and the care of owners or the wisdom of authorities has left it exceptionally free from the blemishes of suburbia. The villages within its boundaries are still villages not only in name but in fact. Industry has left it alone; the only trades that trouble it are those needed to supply its own personal requirements. It bears few of the marks of capitalist exploitation. It has not even attracted the attentions of the catering or amusement purveyors to anything like the normal extent. It is half agricultural, half residential; it has rich and poor, but no very rich, and the poor are not the victims of commercial boom or depression or lack of employment. They have not been organised into distress by industrial magnates or trade union leaders. If a decent life is to be found anywhere, it ought to be obtainable in the Rural District of Godstone.

The new politics has little bearing upon a place like this. Parliamentary discussions ignore it. Political argument leaves it out of account. The arts of government are of less importance than the colour of a sweet pea or the market value of eggs or strawberries.

So that, in looking for a bright spot in the dismal story of public finance, we might with full reason expect to find a sound, healthy, hopeful state of affairs in a place like Godstone. But a first glance at the local accounts is sufficient to dispel our hopes. The new politics has failed to leave even this favoured corner of our green and pleasant land without the universal dread of bankruptcy. Turning first to the published statement of the loans of the Rural District Council, we are brought face to face with our problem in its most vivid and obvious form. It is to be doubted whether more than a few dozen of the 24,696 careless residents of the Godstone area have any knowledge of their personal and corporate indebtedness, or whether more than a small minority have ever bothered to enquire or think about the matter at all. When, now and then, proposals are afoot for street lighting, schools, houses, or sewers, the habit of the people is to talk in terms of a penny rate, for the most outrageous extravagance can be made to assume a false character when reduced to a mere matter of a few pence in the pound. The good people of Godstone may, to some extent, excuse themselves on the ground that indebtedness has never been a question with them, a few years ago there was no indebtedness worth mentioning, and they themselves have not been specially consulted as to the creation of any new liabilities. They know in a general sort of way that Parliament has passed various Acts, and also that the local Council has done its best to obey and apply those measures, but these after all are legal questions over which they appear to have little control and therefore little need to bother. They

are certainly not conscious of any particular
benefit from the operation of the new political
ideas; indeed, they still to some extent resent
the compulsion to stick on stamps and they
grumble with unanimity about rates and taxes.
But then, life must have its little grumbles, and
agitation or excitement is out of keeping with the
spirit of Godstone. The district is predominantly
Conservative, the Tory candidate is not always
opposed, and Socialism is not considered respectable.

Yet the Loans Account of the local Council
reads in all essentials exactly like that of Poplar.
The first item in the current statement shows
that on February 1st, 1901, the District Council
borrowed from the Prudential Assurance Co. the
precise sum of £906 for 30 years at 3¾ per cent. in
respect of its sewage disposal works. The last
instalment of that loan, amounting to £45, is
payable in the year ending March 31st, 1931.
The Council does not owe a penny piece borrowed
before 1901. The Victorians have not left so
much as a farthing rate for the present inhabitants
to discharge.

February 1st, 1901, is a convenient date for
our purposes, coming as it does right at the beginning of the era of the new politics whose costs we
are trying to reckon. Still very largely under the
influence of the ideas of thirty years ago, and
giving little if any more attention to their financial
position than was their habit at that time, the
ratepayers of Godstone will one day wake up to

experience the alarms and sensations familiar to
some of them in other capacities – say as share-
holders in a Hatry company. For the new politics,
the desire to manage and control everybody and
everything, and the determination of Whitehall
to have a finger in every drain in Godstone, has
already put this delightful place on to the very
edge of bankruptcy. Starting with the modest
sum of £906 in 1901, the Council, by March 31st,
1929, had borrowed in all no less a sum than
£436,939. The £906 borrowed with Victorian care
and caution represented a liability of a single
shilling a head of the population, while the
twentieth-century operations of the same character amount to 354 shillings for every man,
woman, and child in the neighbourhood.

Another glance at the Loans Account discloses
another significant change in its character. The
commercial lender like the Royal Liver Friendly
Society still lends money to the Council, but out
of 115 separate loans, all contracted in the last
thirty years, no less than 93 have been provided
by the Public Works Loan Commissioners, Whitehall. This little point is probably more important
than would appear upon the surface. The borrower
does not ordinarily mind very much who is the
lender. So long as the terms are convenient and
reasonable, one lender is, as a general rule, as
good as another.   But that may not be the whole
story. The fundamental facts, if they could be
known, might be of very great importance to our
present enquiry. It is, however, one of the

characteristics of our modern machinery of government that fundamental facts are hard to find,
and that personal knowledge and responsibility
have for all practical purposes been abolished.
But we can picture the careful Rural Councillors
of Godstone in the year 1901 determining that
the sewage disposal works must be put in hand,
and for that purpose driving a business bargain
with the Prudential Assurance Co. at 3¾ per cent.
to lend them £906. And our knowledge of more
modern ways will also enable us to compare that
transaction, thoroughly sound and businesslike
in its character, with the subsequent £436,939.
We can imagine an official of the new Ministry
of Transport summoning the Council to attend
at Whitehall to hear a decision, or a virtual
decision, to widen a road corner at a cost of say
£25,000. We can imagine the modest protests of
the local Councillors and their doubts as to the
need for the widening or the justice of the price,
and we know how such doubts would be brow-
beaten in the impressive atmosphere of the council
chamber of the Ministry. We further know that
Whitehall would flourish Acts of Parliament in the
face of the local deputation, and also that another
set of bureaucrats, the Public Works Loan Commissioners, would force the necessary money
down the throats of the reluctant locality. The
fact that the money for the loan comes out of the
taxpaying pockets of the same ratepayers who
must find the interest is the sort of consideration
which would have weighed with the Rural

Councillor on February 1st, 1901, but is too old-fashioned to mention on March 31st, 1929.

The study of a matter like this is rendered no easier by the thought that the particular proposal may be good in itself. Most of this sort of work has something to be said for it. Whether or not the residents of Godstone are conscious of £436,939 worth of improvement in the amenities of the neighbourhood, it remains true that in the short space of thirty years far more money has been spent by the local authority than the total of all the expenses of all the authorities that have had charge of its affairs in all the centuries since its first Saxon records were written. The greater part of this vast sum has, of course, been expended since the close of an impoverishing war, even Godstone having fallen a victim to the new notion that having suffered heavy loss, we are thus in a position to spend more freely.

It should be stated for the sake of technical accuracy that, although £436,939 has been borrowed and spent on works in the district, the whole of the sum does not fall as a charge upon the rates and some of it has been repaid. £369,490 is the unpaid balance at March 31st, 1929. A closer study of the detailed accounts shows that the Surrey County Council, the Ministries of Transport and Health, the Exchequer and the Ministry of Agriculture have all made grants to the District Council, on which it is permissible to observe that a saving on the Godstone rates is made at a greater cost on the taxes. Whitehall

gets a double interest in these transactions, which
may be necessary but is certainly expensive. The
Public Works Loan Commissioners keep a number
of officers to make loans to Godstone, and the
Ministry of Health keep still more officers to make
grants to help Godstone to pay. Any satisfaction
derived from the thought that the total of the
debt is reduced in this way must be set off against
the knowledge that both the county and the
nation have spent large sums in Godstone which
do not rank as local liabilities. So much for the
capital account of the Rural District of Godstone,
as at March 31st, 1929, a position which continues
to grow more serious as day by day Parliament
and Whitehall impose ever more numerous obligations upon this innocent and unoffending locality.
Godstone is only one of thousands of local
authorities, all of them being in something like
the same position. The local government of this
country is entrusted to 62 county councils, 83
county borough councils, 256 non-county borough
councils, 29 metropolitan borough councils, 783
urban district councils, and 640 rural district
councils, these figures being for England and
Wales. Scotland remains content with a simpler
system of county, burgh, and parish councils,
but if we leave them out of our calculation we
may consider Godstone as typical of 1,813 local
authorities, each of them with similar financial
problems.

Turning from the balance sheet to the revenue
account showing the day by day expenditure
Kʀ

of the Rural District Council, the figures for 1913
and for 1929 are set out in the summary form on
the opposite page. These figures, in their general
characteristics, do not differ from all local and
national statistics. The novelty about them consists in the setting side by side of pre-war and
post-war calculations, a practice which might be
more generally adopted with advantage. It is
probably a new thought to most of the residents
of the Rural District of Godstone that more than
five-sixths of all the activities of their local Council
were not in the catalogue even so recently as 1913.
Seeing that the agitation for more public expenditure grows stronger day by day, and
continues to base its arguments upon the theory
that nothing is done and that capitalism is a
failure, it should be more generally understood
that the socialisation of our wealth and our
incomes has already proceeded a very long way.
Some students of the matter will think that the
experiments made in the last few years are on a
sufficiently large scale to demonstrate the futility
of the method; others will prefer to believe that
all this expenditure represents progress, and to
press for more. Both schools of thought, however,
will be better able to think clearly and argue
logically if they will study comparative figures
such as those given on the opposite page.

It would be hard to find any considerable body
of opinion in Godstone in support of the view
that the local government of 1929 was worth six
times the price of the same sort of government in

	Year ended March 31, 1913			Year ended March 31, 1929		
	£	s.	d.	£	s.	d.
Highways . . .	24,109	18	6	86,494	5	5
Hospitals . . .	1,130	12	2	2,787	12	5
Infectious Disease . .	216	3	9	442	2	1
Commons . . .	2	3	9	71	17	2
Medical Officer of Health and Sanitary Inspector .	—			650	10	0
Housing, Housing Assisted Schemes, Housing Subsidies, Housing Act 1924, and Small Dwellings Loan Account . .	—			27,505	17	0
Salaries, Cost of Rate Collection and Valuation Expenses, Compensation to Displaced Officers and Superannuation . .	1,209	6	5	10,003	17	0
Establishment Charges .	704	2	0	2,073	13	0
Stationery, Printing . .	—			1,183	13	1
National Insurance . .	34	19	11	498	16	6
Town Planning Expenses .	—			371	17	4
Payments to Other Authorities	75	13	7	52,237	3	1
Legal Expenses . .	3,136	1	9	356	18	6
Dust Removal . .	305	2	8	—		
Election Expenses . .	74	2	11	—		
Fire Hydrants . .	67	2	2	—		
Sundries . . .	69	7	8	191	15	8
Waterworks . .	221	4	1	—		
Loans Interest and Repayment	2,776	5	7	—		
Special Expenses Account .	—			13,730	11	4
Sewerage Loan Accounts .	2,289	9	10	10,949	15	8
Crockham Hill Reconstruction	—			8,575	17	6
Total . .	£36,421	16	9	£218,126	2	9

NOTE.—Differences in keeping and rendering the accounts in the two periods make exact comparisons of any item difficult. For instance, "Loan Interest and Repayment" is now calculated in the cost of the housing or other scheme concerned. Similarly the salaries of officers account for more than the £10,003 shown above, because some of these payments are allocated to departments. While, therefore, the totals of this account are accurate according to the published figures, any argument based upon the details would require supporting with more complete information.

1913. The £36,421 of 1913 was spent on account of a population of 34,158, and represented an expenditure per head of 21s. 3d., but the £218,126 of 1929 is chargeable to 24,696 persons, and amounts to 176s. 7d. per head, or more than eight times the previous figure. Since 1913 Godstone has lost the parish of Caterham, with a population of 10,841, and five of the fourteen parishes which remain have actually decreased in the numbers of their inhabitants. The outstanding difference between the two periods, so far as any practical difference is to be found, is in the condition of the roads, which are now very greatly improved. Here again there will be two points of view. Those who believe that the expenditure of vast sums on road schemes is helpful in a period of unemployment will applaud the self-sacrifice of the ratepayers of Godstone. The opposite view, which holds that forced expenditure through public authorities with money taken from private resources handicaps trade and creates unemployment, will lead others to regret that all this road expenditure should have been pressed forward immediately after an impoverishing war, and to attribute to it a full share of our commercial and industrial difficulties.

These accounts make it clear that we must expect to find a considerable increase in the number of officials employed by the District Council, and the published records give ample support to that conclusion. In the following table we set out side by side the various offices, with the

salaries attached to them and the names of their
holders.

A satisfactory study of this impressive list is
impossible without a much fuller understanding
of the work and functions of a Rural District
Council than most of the ratepayers possess.
All these officials have, no doubt, something to
do with Godstone, but are in practice much more
concerned with Kingston and, through Kingston,
with Whitehall. Nine-tenths of their functions
are duplicated at the offices of the Surrey County
Council at Kingston, and most of the functions
of both Godstone and Kingston are performed
over again by the Whitehall staff of the Ministry
of Health, by the Ministry of Transport, or by
one or other of the Government departments
claiming to exercise jurisdiction over the well-
being of Godstone. A very large proportion of
the time of the persons named in the following
schedule is therefore occupied first in seeking
approval or permission from Kingston and Whitehall and then reporting back to these superior
authorities on action taken in pursuance of such
permission.

Godstone, as I have said, is a very desirable
part of the world, and it is not therefore surprising
to find that it is served by a body of bureaucrats
who are just as nice as it is possible for bureaucrats
to be. But when it becomes necessary for one of
the ratepayers of Godstone to spend half an hour
in the Council offices, seeking permission to build
a chicken-run or follow some other normal human

SALARIES OF OFFICERS OF THE RURAL DISTRICT COUNCIL OF GODSTONE

Officer	1913 Name	1913 Salary [1]	1929 Name	1929 Salary
		£ s. d.		£ s. d.
Clerk of the Council	E. A. Head	350 0 0	C. Phillips	505 0 0
Assistant Clerk	C. Phillips	10 0 0	F. W. Walpole	275 0 0
2nd Assistant Clerk	—		W. J. Maskell	200 0 0
Accounts Clerk	—		F. W. Sewell	170 0 0
Office Clerk	—		S. V. Halsey	160 0 0
Highways Costing Clerk	—		H. E. Garman	140 0 0
Office Clerk	—		H. Light	130 0 0
Office Clerk (General Office)	—		E. A. Beaumont	90 0 0
Office Clerk (General Office)	—		A. A. Crowhurst	52 0 0
Office Boy (General Office)	—		H. J. Perryman	39 0 0
Typist	—		A. G. Hannan	150 0 0
Typist	—		H. K. Hooker	150 0 0
Typist	—		M. Dove	150 0 0
Rating and Valuation Officer	—		S. A. Wright	295 0 0
Assistant to Rating and Valuation Officer	—		D. Jarvis	130 0 0
Rating Officer:				
Northern Area	—		H. T. E. Jarrett	372 0 0
Southern Area	—		F. Selby	220 0 0
Eastern Area	—		W. H. Wood	225 0 0
Western Area	—		A. W. Eddolls	200 0 0
Bletchingley Parish	—		B. Ashdown	150 0 0
Highways Surveyor and Director of Town Planning	G. E. Crowter	250 0 0	G. E. Crowter	750 0 0
Assistant Highways Surveyor	—		R. V. Crook	270 0 0
2nd Assistant Highways Department	—		F. Marchant	180 0 0
Articled Pupil, Highways Department	—		G. Legg	80 0 0
Storekeeper, Highways Depot, Godstone	—		W. Wisden	104 0 0
Chief Town Planning Assistant	—		G. W. G. Wilks	270 0 0
Junior Town Planning Assistant	—		W. M. Houston	120 0 0
Buildings Surveyor	T. C. Barralet [2]	275 0 0	S. F. Evershed	450 0 0
Assistant to Buildings Surveyor	H. W. Lovelock	91 0 0	E. Brackfield	260 0 0

[1] Per annum except where otherwise stated.

[2] Styled "Sanitary and Buildings Surveyor" in 1913.

Officer	1913 Name	1913 Salary¹ £ s. d.	1929 Name	1929 Salary £ s. d.
Buildings Inspector	—	—	N. Humphrey	210 0 0
Assistant in Buildings Department	John E. Hopcraft	6 0 per week	W. R. Hand	230 0 0
Consulting Surveyor			T. C. Barralet	208 0 0
Medical Officer of Health	Dr. F. W. Robertson	130 0 0	W. H. Butcher	330 0 0
Sanitary Inspector	George H. Widger²	175 0 0	C. F. Payne	300 0 0
Other Duties of Sanitary Inspector	—		C. F. Payne	50 0 0
Assistant to Sanitary Inspector	Edred Weeks	65 0 0	A. G. Thomas	190 0 0
Office Clerk, Sanitary Department	Miss Steer	1 0 0 per week	A. H. Sewell	70 0 0
Inspector under the Petroleum Acts	Talbot Kyle	15 0 0 per week	Talbot Kyle	28 0 0
Deputy Medical Officer of Health			P. C. V. Bent	31 10 0
ISOLATION HOSPITAL.				
Medical Officer	—		W. H. Butcher	150 0 0
Matron	—		J. D. Smith	105 0 0
Staff Nurse	—		D. Passby	55 0 0
Staff Nurse	—		D. Richardson	61 0 0
Assistant Nurse	—		H. E. Hiscock	51 0 0
Assistant Nurse	—		E. Lusher	45 0 0
Probationer Nurse	—		J. John	35 0 0
Probationer Nurse	—		D. Hemmings	35 0 0
Cook	—		N. Wheatley	40 0 0
Housemaid	—		B. Spragg	32 0 0
Wardsmaid	—		D. Orchard	32 0 0
Wardsmaid	—		O. Woods	32 0 0
Laundress	—		Mrs. Pearson	5 per day
Porter, Manager, Tilburstow Hill Pits, and Assistant to Surveyor	W. Wisden	120 0 0	G. Allen	132 3 4
Temporary Engineering Assistant	W. H. Tolcher	100 0 0	—	
Office Clerk	A. Denny	10 0 0 per week	—	

1 Per annum except where otherwise stated. 2 Styled "Inspector of Nuisances" in 1913.

desire, that ratepayer leaves the offices, notwithstanding the personal charm of the officials,
either wondering what it is all about, or boiling
with indignation at the injustice put upon him.
These officials are the tools of Whitehall. They
are the minor instruments of "the New
Despotism" so graphically described by Lord
Hewart. They try to be as polite and agreeable
as possible to the residents of Godstone, but it
hardly ever enters their heads that they exist for
the convenience or comfort of those residents,
or that the views and opinions of the individual
ratepayers are worth even thinking about. When
a resident of the district calls upon them to
report that, having bought an Austin Seven, he
proposes to enlarge his cycle shed, they are full of
sympathy. They almost apologise while they
explain that the plans must be submitted to the
building department and, if they survive that
process, must then be copied again for the edifica-
tion of the town planning officer, and subsequently
examined with a view to the reassessment of the
property as a whole. They are full of sympathy
when the ratepayer tells of his journeyings to
other authorities for registration numbers, car
licences, and driver's licences. They regret that
they cannot say what is likely to be the effect of
the proposed addition to the cycle shed upon the
assessments to income tax for Schedule A or B.
Those matters are outside their jurisdiction. They
agree that the proposed assessment of the shed
will involve a readjustment of the charges for

water, but, like every other of the numerous
governmental complications involved in the purchase of an Austin Seven, they are in no way
responsible. They are merely performing their
duty in accordance with "the Act." The word
"Act" will be spoken in a conclusive tone of
respect as if they were speaking of the Acts of
the Apostles. Their minds are full of the schedules
which they must send to their superiors of the
County Council, and the ratepayer is a cipher to
appear in the appropriate column. Most of the
time of these people is occupied in passing forms
to and from Godstone to Kingston, and Godstone
to Whitehall, and a good deal of their work consists of visits to those places. They get really busy
when some new Act redistributes their functions
and moves the jurisdiction over paupers or roads
from one authority to another. Shutting up
Guardians and arranging for the work to be done
some other and some more expensive way is one
of their favourite occupations, and they are
experts in checking and auditing and "making
observations" on one another's work.

It remains to observe, in considering the
machinery of government as applied to Godstone,
that a study of the doings of the Rural District
Council by no means exhausts the subject. There
are numerous public functions which still remain
outside the jurisdiction of the local Council, and
the cost of this body and its official machinery
is only a part of the price which the residents pay
for the privilege of citizenship under modern

conditions. The administration of justice and the police force provide their necessary quota of non-producers sharing with the rest the wealth and produce of the whole. But in addition we have to allow for labour exchanges, customs and excise, income tax officers, clerks to licensing justices, education officers, inspectors of weights and measures, inspectors of licences for dogs and guns, the persons responsible for the administration of pensions, of factory Acts, agricultural lecturers and inspectors, slaughter-house regulators, inspectors under the food and drugs Acts, to mention only a few of the people who claim an interest in Godstone on behalf of various Government departments.

If we turn to the county as distinct from the rural district or the national administration, we find that in the Surrey County Hall there are 700 clerks and officials, or twice the number of policemen of all ranks in the Surrey Constabulary.

Thus even such superficial examination of the matter as is alone possible in this connection gives us a very impressive picture of the effects of the new politics on a little place like Godstone in so short a period as the seventeen years between 1913 and 1929. Our present purpose is not so much to argue as to the wisdom or folly of what has been done as to suggest that a more general knowledge of the amount and the cost of it all would help to promote wisdom in any further discussion of these matters.

CHAPTER XII

THE NATION'S CAPITAL ACCOUNT

FAILURE to appreciate the difference between capital and income is the easiest and most dangerous of the pitfalls that beset the path of the private individual or the business concern. The speculative company promoter fattens on this failure. When an industrial undertaking gets into his hands, he will charge to capital many things that wiser people would charge to income, and thus, for the purpose of the flotation that he has in view, will swell the assets as well as the profits to make them both appear better than they really are, and appear to justify the inflated price at which the public will buy the concern. A business, on the other hand, which belongs to people gifted with financial wisdom, will be careful to regard every possible expense as a charge on income, and will debit the capital account only with such expenditure as can really be regarded as a permanent addition to the assets of the concern.

The maintenance of the capital of the private person, of the business concern, or of the nation is quite vital to its economic well-being. But, from a long tradition which need not be discussed in this connection, the nation has no capital account. The annual Budget is a record of the incomings and the outgoings, a mere cash account,

and there is nowhere in the Treasury ledgers
anything which would exactly correspond to the
capital account of the private individual. No
figures are put against Government buildings
or the furniture in them. The ships of the Navy
or the guns of the Army are not entered up and
carried forward as worth so much. And thus it
comes about that the actual value at any given
moment of the nation's capital is unknown. The
modern State, with the single exception of Russia,
is run upon the theory that the citizens will be
wealthy enough to meet its obligations. Its capital
consists of the taxable capacity of its members,
but, unlike its members, it has not constantly
before it an account marked "capital," and is
unable to watch from day to day or from year to
year the growth or the diminution of that account.
When a private individual sells his house and the
price – say £1,000 – goes into his bank, he sometimes finds it a little difficult to make his family
understand that this sudden accession to the bank
balance is not an adequate justification for fur
coats all round. The house is a lasting asset, and
must be replaced by a lasting asset. To exchange
a house with a life of sixty or eighty years for a
fur coat with a life of three or four years is to
exchange a capital value for something which is
of a very different nature.

No such restraining thought troubles the mind
of the Chancellor of the Exchequer when he
collects the death-duties, two or three hundred
millions of the nation's capital values, and

proceeds to spend that money on a battleship which will be out of date in a few years, or on a dole which will in practice ruin the capital-creating qualities of the people who receive it.

There are grave difficulties in these days, when the nation has thought it well to adopt a spendthrift policy, in discussing such a vital but abstruse problem as the difference between income and capital. The difficulties are made the greater by the undoubted fact that for the moment many of us appear to be rather better off than before, and, having very superficial knowledge of these matters, most of us decide that we can safely leave the experts to find some way out, and that there is no particular reason why we should worry. That view is adopted almost with unanimity by the politicians who, tempted by the popularity bought by money which ought never to be spent, continue to offer the people more and more, and drag them farther down the slope towards bankruptcy. The Victorian Member of Parliament who from his own pocket paid £5 apiece for votes was bad enough, but the modern M.P. who has heaped a debt of £500 on each of us for the same unworthy purpose is infinitely worse.

Present tendencies, bad as they are, can be made the basis of either pessimism or hope. The pessimists take the view that we are as certain of extinction as was the Roman Empire in the second century, and assume that the nation will go on wasting its capital, squandering the savings of the past, and leaving posterity to face the inevitable ruin. The optimists, on the other hand, think rather better of British democracy, and there are ample grounds for this more hopeful view. Thirty million electors are given responsibility for the preservation of the nation's capital. Most of them have no personal experience to guide them. Their knowledge of finance is limited to so many shillings a week. Very few of these people, by the nature of things, have any prospect during their little lives of writing their names on a cheque for £100. In these circumstances the optimists, the true believers in democracy, are surely justified in the theory that our people possess a solid, inherent sense of right, and that the extravagance which we see all around us is only a passing post-war phase which might have been much worse and the end of which is beginning to be in sight. That end will be hastened when we see more clearly the future damage that must result from our present actions.

In deference to the tradition that an account should contain figures, it may be well to give a sample or two to show the sort of thing that is happening. Figures appeal to some minds; others prefer to rely upon deeper indications of essential things.

The Westminster Bank *Circular* for August, 1930, dealt at length with the national debts of various countries, and, expressing the post-war as a percentage of the pre-war figures, taking the pre-war to be 100, showed that the post-war debt of Great Britain is 787 against 100, of France is 145 against 100, and of Italy is 106 against 100. These comparisons deal only with the actual national debt, and ignore local obligations; they deal only with official figures, and ignore all the undisclosed liabilities which, as we have seen, amount to even more. But even these inadequate figures bring out very clearly how we have arranged for our children to carry the burden. When we turn from national to local debts the story is as bad, and illustrates the moral responsibility of Parliament in relation to the general question of extravagance. When Parliament squanders money every local authority proceeds to do the same, and, strangely enough, the individuals on whom both rely are caught up in the same profligate wave. So that not only does the national account considered by itself become weaker; the local accounts get bankrupt and the private accounts on which both rely go from bad to worse. Liverpool is a typical example of the story to be found in any of our towns or counties. The gross debt of Liverpool on March 31st, 1930, was £56,023,478. This enormous total is diminished by the allocation of nearly half of it to what are called "trading" or "reproductive" services. Seeing, however, that most of these debts were in respect of services established or plant bought in the most expensive post-war market, the original £56,000,000 is probably nearer to the actual liability of the citizens than the lower figure of £35,424,203 which the city accountants admit to exist without any corresponding assets to balance it. The gross local debt of the citizen of Liverpool, including every man, woman, and child, is £60 per head, which compares with £17 in 1913. If this be added to the share of the National Debt which each citizen of Liverpool must shoulder, no doubt can exist as to the bankruptcy of Liverpool, for the most ardent admirer of that progressive city would not claim tangible assets amounting to hundreds of pounds for every soul who lives there. It will be agreed by most people that all this expenditure is undertaken in the anticipation that the rate and taxpayers will have sufficient means to meet it when the bills come due. But, while we work upon this assumption, the public policy of every party, as expressed in the actions of every Chancellor of the Exchequer, is to weaken these same taxpayers on whose security the whole scheme relies. One Chancellor will take it to his credit that he has eliminated a wealthy class; others will pretend to have the interests of the taxpayer at heart. It makes no difference. One after another they invent some fresh turn of the screw, driving the taxpayer out of the region of sound finance. The last Budget has produced a state of affairs in which the very wealthy man must in any case spend his life in watching his estate diminish. *The Times* City Notes give us a table showing that a person with a gross capital of £1,000,000 and a gross income of £50,000 is absolutely prevented from maintaining that estate and handing it on to his wife and family. The income tax, surtax, and insurance premium to provide for death-duty on such an estate amount to £52,837 per annum, and the capital of £1,000,000 must therefore diminish year by year by at least £2,837. No great enthusiasm can perhaps be developed on behalf of the individual who possesses a million, and if the case against taxation rested upon the views or wishes of this person alone it would not be worth arguing. But when we remember that the lavish expenditure of the City of Liverpool and of every city and parish in the land, added to the ever-growing national burdens, is all undertaken on the assumption that this million will continue to exist, and will continue to provide huge tax revenues, the millionaire becomes a national asset instead of a political bogey. But the use of the millionaire goes far beyond his possibilities as a taxpayer. It is on him that we rely to provide our industrial development. Nobody can calculate the loss we have suffered in recent years because of the weakening of the ability of the millionaires to finance new industries.

I am not an expert in the cinema business, but it will serve me as an illustration. I know nothing whatever about the difficulties of the British film as against the American or the German. I do know that if I am tempted to visit a picture theatre I must suffer the offence to my national pride and artistic taste of witnessing American notions of humour expressed in English which

LR

has suffered from lack of contact with the source
of the language. I strongly suspect, however,
that if any one of the first five thousand of our
super-taxpayers had been in a position to put
his taxes into the English cinema industry, the
Americans would not now possess a virtual
monopoly of that market, and the cinema might
to-day be an influence for good. This business, a
typical victim of the national financial policy of
the time, has come upon a market without the
proper means to provide sound finance for pioneer
work. It has, perforce, been largely left to professional financiers working with the money of
the speculative middle-class public; it has been
subject to all the booms and slumps of the Stock
Exchange, and run on a basis which, to a large
extent, precludes personal financial responsibility.
Had some millionaire been in a position to use
his own money, and to bring to the service of the
cinema all the care and economy and caution
of personal ownership; been able to nurse a
loss in the old-fashioned way (for a loss is often
the basis of great success in the hands of the
man who actually suffers it himself), I can
imagine that this country might be giving the
world the benefit of English ideas on the cinema
screen.

A very great deal of nonsense is talked about
capital expenditure. Much of our educational
extravagance is sometimes supported on the
grounds that the children are the nation's capital.
The children will in due course need to possess

generous qualities to avoid a certain cynicism and bitterness when they repeat this phrase. No previous experience exists to guide us as to what is likely to happen to a country with an educated proletariat who are without the means to lead a civilised life. If the notion of economy comes back into our public affairs without much further delay, we can at least have the satisfaction of doing something to minimise the difficulties of the future. Some people think that education will lead us to the simple life; those folk are certainly doing their best to force the simple life upon us. Meantime the fact remains that we are spending the savings of the past; that we are stopping up the possibility of saving in the present; and that we are mortgaging the savings of the future. All these things arise from our failure to appreciate the necessity for the existence of a national capital account. Macaulay, in his essay on Southey's *Colloquies*, gave us a passage which exactly fits the present position: "But what is useful expenditure? 'A liberal expenditure in national works,' says Mr. Southey, 'is one of the surest means for promoting national prosperity.' What does he mean by national prosperity? Does he mean the wealth of the State? If so, his reasoning runs thus: The more wealth a State has the better; for the more wealth a State has the more wealth it will have. . . .If by national prosperity he means the wealth of the people, of how gross a contradiction is Mr. Southey guilty. A people, he tells us, may be too rich: a

Government cannot: for a Government can employ its riches in making the people richer. The wealth of the people is to be taken from them, because they have too much, and laid out in works, which will yield them more."

CHAPTER XIII

PRUDENCE AND ENERGY

BOTH prudence and energy occupy lower places in our minds than they did with the Victorians. Energy is more talked about than practised, and prudence (an unfortunate word with a sort of crinoline flavour) is now seldom mentioned. Yet it is upon the prudence and energy of the people that their well-being entirely depends, and fashion in conversation does not alter basic truth. Seeing that the State has long ago abandoned prudence, and seeing, further, that the quality of energy is from the nature of things absent from an abstract entity such as a State, it is perhaps not surprising that prudence and energy count for less to-day with the average man than was the case thirty years ago. A State can organise, which means nothing more than the creation on paper of a lot of machinery, giving a false appearance of energy without producing the practical results always associated with energy as a personal quality.

Thanks to the Victorians, we are, or were, a very wealthy people, and the loss of both prudence and energy is one of the risks always associated with a condition of wealth. It is a risk which can only be avoided by the exercise of much forethought, and hard forethinking is not a characteristic of the present generation. The Victorians, who practised in their family affairs the principles they applied to national concerns, knew a great deal about the risks of wealth and comfort and ease. Every town and countryside could furnish examples of families going up and others going down. There is no more worthy or anxious task for the head of a family than the rearing of a generation with the knowledge, the wisdom, and the experience, to benefit from the work of the past, while also contributing its own quota towards the building up of the family as an institution. In private affairs the legal device of a life tenancy of an estate is a guard against the risk that the owners for the time being might not be strong enough to resist the temptation to squander its capital values. We badly need to-day a national revival of the conception of life tenancy, for we are only the life tenants of our national heritage. No legal device can help a nation which makes its own laws, especially a nation which has acquired the habit of making new laws from week to week in the stupid hope of curing new troubles, most of which have arisen from the laws of the weeks before. The life tenancy in private affairs has to some extent lost its value as a safeguard, because, however careful the life tenant of an estate may be, the Exchequer, with its death-duties, will squander the capital which the careful tenant has made it the object of his life to preserve. Every private estate is now subject to the devastating operations of spendthrift Governments. Whereas previously family property would increase and diminish and, on balance, the nation had the satisfaction of seeing a general tendency upwards, now the deliberate policy of the modern State is to force the results, if not the character, of a prodigal administration upon all private estates.

Were it possible, as some may once have hoped, that this wholesale transfer from private to public hands would still leave us with our national property intact, it would be harder to take exception to the process. But when we examine the Account Rendered and find not only that private estates have perforce to disappear, but that the national estate is run upon the policy that the life tenants of the future shall pay for the comfort of the present, then indeed prudence does seem to have been forgotten and energy to be no longer worth while.

The attempt to draw a comparison between ourselves and the Victorians is full of interest, and, to judge by present tendencies in thought and literature, is likely to become a popular exercise. A big field for research is opened to the student who feels inclined to enquire into the difference between the character of the public work of those times and these. Most of the great men whose names will be remembered in connection with the social life of the nineteenth century were engaged upon movements which relied entirely upon the qualities and activities of individuals, and were almost invariably recommended to those individuals for free acceptance

or rejection. The very few great names in the field
of social reform during the last thirty years that
will go down to history are all associated with
the opposite notion. Their work has consisted
in the crushing of individuality, and their great-
ness in the extent to which they have succeeded
in this anti-social endeavour. Robert Raikes,
Andrew Carnegie, Passmore Edwards, Wilfrid
Lawson, George Cadbury, George Jacob Holy-
oake, even William Morris, none of them went
to Parliament on behalf of the cause he espoused.
All of them tried to do something to make life
better by complete reliance upon the freewill and
energy of the individual. Now freewill and energy
have given place to force and law, not because
we like force applied to ourselves, but to satisfy
our degrading love of the notion of applying force
to others. Pride in our freedom has given way to
arrogance in power with disastrous consequences
to economic well-being. For freedom engenders
activity.

The force method is helped along from behind
by the incidental consideration that the exercise
of power always means the employment of a
salaried officer.

Force is sometimes applied to the object of the
movement but always to the financing of it. The
Victorians were free to make use or not of the
penny reading; we are equally free to absent
ourselves from the municipal library, but we
are not free to escape the penny rate.

The pride and family love which we freely

mixed together in a provident institution or friendly society, and the energy and effort which we voluntarily applied to such institutions, have given way to a sullen and uneconomic obedience to law which substitutes penalties for pride and adhesive stamps for family love.

The freedom which gave scope for the expression of genuine citizenship in the Band of Hope movement, is now an apathetic slavery to schedules and boundaries and hours.

The free and active co-operation in an effort to run a better grocery store is now to become a soulless machine for bulk purchase by government and ration cards for the citizen. The nineteenth century was characterised by the appeal to individual endeavour. The twentieth, so far, has witnessed nothing but the stupid attempt to suppress individuality by political force.

Passing to the more practical application of the two mentalities to trade and industry, the difference is even more marked. In the nineteenth century everybody knew that the restraint of trade was illegal. The common law left no doubt about the matter, and the common law was rigorously applied. The twentieth century, however, gives us every morning in our newspapers fresh examples of the fashionable mania for the restraint of trade. If the reader will look at the summary of the news of the day in the newspaper for any week he cares to select in the late eighties or early nineties, he cannot fail to notice the strong contrast between those columns and the corresponding columns in any week in recent years. To-day it is hard to find an item that does not concern the deliberations of collectivist bodies engaged in restraining some sort of action or individual. There is no room to-day in the summary of the news for the achievements of ordinary persons in the ordinary work of life, and yet forty years ago the same summaries, of equal interest to a previous generation, knew nothing of committees and commissions, but told us only of the triumphs of the individual man. The nineteenth century understood and insisted that the business of industry was to deliver the goods. The twentieth century gives the best of its brains to devices for restraining production, rationing supplies, and restricting the interchange of commodities.

Another branch of enquiry into this reversal of thought and alteration of character might lead us to consider the difference in our social intercourse one with the other in these two periods. We were always a sociable people. The Englishman loves a crowd; he likes to be among his fellows. That is one reason why he preferred the factory to the farm. The reign of Victoria saw the establishment of all sorts of institutes, societies, and associations for social betterment. They covered every class of object and subject, and ranged from penny readings to royal societies. But, search as we will, there was never any departure in any of these associations from the principle of liberty, nor was there any failure to respect the right of the individual to think and

act for himself. All these movements depended
for their success upon their freedom, and for that
very reason gathered to themselves men of energy
and enthusiasm, both qualities being attributes
of freedom. The twentieth century, on the other
hand, has seen the growth of a much larger group
of associations of various kinds, all of them
founded upon the notion of force, all of them aim-
ing at legislative power which will enable them
to exercise collective authority and suppress
individual freedom.

The Victorians relied upon personal responsibility, personal risk. We set little store by either,
and find a momentary comfort and ease in a sort
of economic morphia, administered by the State.
The spirit of adventure and speculation which
led the Victorians by the hundred thousand into
personal risk and endeavour has been largely
supplanted by the twentieth century safety first
idea. The lengths to which this can be carried was
illustrated at a recent meeting of an urban district
council. With all the false safeguards without
which we do not seem able to move, the council,
after months of deliberation, decided upon the
building of a few houses. But, the decision having
been taken, the work was delayed for another
month while some of the super safety-firsters
succeeded in maintaining a debate as to what
provision should be made in the event of unemployment arising in the neighbourhood among the
men who would be employed to build these houses.
These councillors were saturated so thoroughly

with the safety-first obsession that they hesitated
to begin on work for the reason that it might, one
day, be finished. Could anything be more absurd?
And yet this hesitancy is altogether typical of
the committee age in which we are doomed to live.

The nineteenth century recognised and encouraged inequality, and by loading responsibility
on the shoulders of the individual gave him the
opportunity to show that he was worthy to rise.
The twentieth century has invented an equality
which does not, of course, exist, and has heaped
upon this false foundation a collection of rights
which are fraught with moral disaster far out-
weighing their temporary economic value. In
addition, it has for the moment so arranged and
complicated its affairs that hardly anybody has
any responsibility for anything. Where there is
no responsibility, there is little chance for prudence
and energy.

We have produced a care-free generation with
no adequate conception of the difficulties of providing a civilised life. It is pathetic to witness all
around us men and women with education, some
of them having real brains, who have no higher
ambition than a minor post in the Civil Service
or Imperial Chemical Industries, and who never
for a moment contemplate for themselves the
acceptance of any personal responsibility or risk.
It cannot surely be long before our statesmen and
our politicians will be ready to move on to higher
ground and develop minds which can rise above
a few coppers a week on a particular dole schedule

or 5 per cent. on a particular import, and will talk
to us with some of the old inspiration on a subject
like individual responsibility. Any doubt as to the
need for such a revival can be dispelled at once
by a few enquiries in any branch of modern
endeavour. Ask a tradesman about the price of
an article and he will tell you that the association
has fixed it. He is sorry, he would like to make it
less, but he cannot get supplies unless he conforms
to the rules and regulations. Offer a workman in
a centre where trade unionism is strong a little
less or even a little more than some schedule price.
He will disclaim all responsibility in the matter
and be content to remain a soulless cog in a
mechanical society. Ask the treasurer of your
county council about the rates and he will tell
you that 70 or 80 per cent. of the money that he
has to collect is collected against his will, imposed
upon him by Parliament or by departmental
order, and is quite outside the jurisdiction of the
council. Ask Whitehall, and you will be told that
the local authority is the cause of the trouble.
Ask Parliament, and you will be referred back to
Whitehall. Go back and complain in Whitehall,
and you will be told that Parliament is to blame.
It is the exception rather than the rule to-day
to be able to track down even a little bit of evil
to the fault or failure of a particular individual.
Responsibility has become an impersonal thing, or,
or it would be more correct to say, has disappeared.

The twentieth century is the period of the
triumph of politics, a triumph which must surely

be a short-lived one, with very salutary lessons for the future. In all material matters the futility of the political method as against the individualist plan is demonstrated beyond question. The Government runs our telephones, and while, because England has not yet lost all those qualities of efficiency and skill which the Victorians invented, the telephone works fairly well, we are nevertheless the most under-telephoned people in civilisation. We come twenty-third on the list of countries in the number of telephones per head of the population, and the simple and only reason is that every telephone has to submit to the natural hindrance due to the absence of any personal responsibility. The telephone employee is a Civil Servant and free from the risk of discharge. But what applies to telephones applies equally to every Government action. A far worse case, and one for which we shall pay more dearly, is our plight in the matter of education, simply because we are still under the impression that a Parliamentary or Governmental method is capable of functioning satisfactorily. What a different record might have been made if our super-tax-payers had been left in their private capacities to care for higher education, as has been done in, say, America or Sweden! The United States, with less than a quarter of our personal taxation, boasts 600 universities, with three quarters of a million university students and £110,000,000 of endowments.[1] In Iowa alone there are as many

[1] *Columbus, Undergraduate :* J. A. Benn.

university students as in the whole of England, although the population is only 2,000,000. The standard may not be as high as ours, but we have had a few centuries' start in the matter. It is interesting to notice that in the United States, although the forty-eight legislatures, corresponding in some ways to our county councils, do a good deal in the matter of education, no federal authority, no Whitehall, overrules the educational efforts of any State. Imagination boggles at the possibilities for good for the world as a whole if such educational opportunities as have been available in the United States in the last thirty years had been applied to the English character. The Victorians, without any education, dragged themselves and the whole of the world from a condition which was almost as near to barbarism as at the time of the Normans up to a condition of civilisation such as we know to-day. If England in the twentieth century had, like America, used business brains and local freedom, both spurred on by competition, in the service of education, we might as we stand to-day have had to our credit an even more glorious revolution in the standard of life and living. Our sense of responsibility towards mankind has degenerated into filling the world with committees and bureaucrats under a banner with the strange device: "Self-determination." We need more self-determination for the individual, and less for the collection of individuals known as the State.

"It is not by the intermeddling of . . . the

omniscient and omnipotent State, but by the prudence and energy of the people, that England has hitherto been carried forward in civilisation; and it is to the same prudence and the same energy that we now look with comfort and good hope. Our rulers will best promote the improvement of the nation by strictly confining themselves to their own legitimate duties, by leaving capital to find its most lucrative course, commodities their fair price, industry and intelligence their natural reward, idleness and folly their natural punishment, by maintaining peace, by defending property, by diminishing the price of law, and by observing strict economy in every department of the State. Let the Government do this: the people will assuredly do the rest."[1]

[1] Macaulay : *Essays.*

CHAPTER XIV

KNAVES AND FOOLS

THE perfect State would consist of a society where all obey and none command. There liberty and justice would prevail, and law would be relegated to the position in which Timothy places it, and would be concerned with the small class of liars and perjurers. In that perfect State law would be supported by unanimous public opinion, and law so supported would enforce itself. When law has behind it the conscious sanction and consent of the people, the individual man runs the risk of losing the esteem of his friends and neighbours if he fail to observe it. The outstanding illustration of the other sort of law is prohibition in the United States, which (whether it be good or bad is beside the question) is so far ahead of a large mass of public opinion as to need an army of spies to make its purpose even partially effective.

The period of the new politics, which has produced two laws a week, lifts these considerations out of the realm of the practical. It is obviously impossible to develop public opinion fast enough to secure its force behind so great a mass of legislation. When the new politics, with all its attendant damage, has run its course, and after the stock-taking which is now beginning is complete, people will take a wiser view of these matters and realise that a society can only absorb a new law now and again, and our practice will be to limit the operations of the legislature to a maximum of one Act of Parliament a year.

The confusion, muddle, and contradiction which arise from the rage for legislation make up between them a very heavy debit item in the account which we are engaged in rendering to ourselves. The loss and destruction directly due to our self-conceit in thinking that we can regulate the affairs of everybody must be set against the wealth and comfort which were brought into the world by the operation of the opposite ideas of the Victorians who believed in *laisser faire*. Volumes could be written to show how Acts of Parliament contradict one another, how one defeats the purpose of another, and how impossible it is in many circumstances to conform to one without infringing the stipulations of another. We are constantly compelled to choose between the sin of exceeding the speed limit and the felony of failing to deposit our plans in triplicate on linen paper edged with pink at the appropriate office within the seven days prescribed by the Act which allows us to do something else. A grotesque example of this sort of thing was given to us in the case of the Swan & Edgar building in Piccadilly Circus, where one set of Government inspectors insisted upon an extra storey to satisfy one of the many conditions of the London Building Act and another public office, strangely enough under the control of the same Ministry, declined to pass this extra Parliamentary storey because it could not be made to conform to another enactment supposed to be concerned with the people's safety. The area of self-government in man's personal affairs is steadily and rapidly diminishing. Day by day, as the machinery of organisation, both official and unofficial, develops, there remains less and less that the individual is able either in his actions or his property to regard as within his personal disposition.

If we add to all the legislation of the last thirty years the programmes of the political parties for the next few years, and remember that the admitted complications of the old legislation and the additional intricacies which the new will introduce will all be further complicated by departmental phraseology expressed in sub-clauses which few can find and nobody can understand, we get an inkling of the troubles which confront the modern business man. Stability, as that quality was understood fifty years ago, no longer exists to-day. Three, and five, and seven year contracts for the supply of materials and commodities were the commonplaces of business up to the eighties, and contained within their terms all that security of employment, confidence, and certainty, the absence of which is the chief of our difficulties to-day.

In rendering our account we have to recognise that the new politics, the social-reform-by-Act-of-Parliament idea, has brought about a radical change in the character of law itself. The very meaning of the word has altered. Law used to be conceived as an arrangement by means of which society was able to deal with evildoers. Now, law falls on the just and unjust alike, but chiefly on the just. Modern law can be defined as an arrangement whereby the every action of everybody, from the cradle to the grave, is entered upon a card index. We have produced a state of affairs when it is comparatively unimportant how you get into the cradle or how you go into the grave, but it is of vital importance that, when performing either operation or any little act in between the two, you should have with you the appropriate official chits and forms. The birth of a Victorian was registered once, and that formality was not always observed. The modern father must chase after two separate Government departments, fill up forms in triplicate and between the prescribed hours, not for his convenience or comfort, but in order that the various bureaucrats whose salaries and pensions are even more dear to Whitehall than the happiness of the infant concerned, may upon the information received continue to be a nuisance both to the child and to the father. Thereafter whenever the child desires to build a chicken-house, to have a drink, to cross the Channel, to ride a motor-bicycle, to put a shilling on a horse, to attend a concert, to photograph his mother, or to buy a box of pills, he will find there is a bureaucrat in the background drawing a salary for limiting his liberty in these and almost all other matters.

When this dreadful period is over and our

children have recognised that there are better purposes in life than framing Acts of Parliament, they will see more clearly that progress is in inverse ratio to the coercive interference of man with man. They may even be wise enough to know that progress is in direct ratio to the free play upon man of natural and external forces. Then there will be a sudden reversal of all the machinery for relieving us from the inconveniences of the laws of nature, the futility and damage of any such attempt being obvious to all.

The Englishman of the future will be, like his Victorian forbears, a much humbler creature than the Englishman of the present. He will enjoy an intellectual humility which will permit of a resumption of pride in virtue, work, and effort. To-day this quality is at a discount, and we are afflicted with a very troublesome form of intellectual snobbery. The fashion for coercive interference arises from the priggish conceit, fostered and encouraged by the new politics, that all wrong is done by somebody else, and that we, being right, are capable not only of recognising the wrong, not only of tracking down the very fellow who is doing it, but also of putting him right. The whole conception is shallow and full of personal vanity. It ignores all available human experience, it constitutes a grave threat to the civilisation that previous generations have bequeathed to us, and the end of it cannot be much longer delayed.

To think that it is possible to level up by

legislation is to ignore the levelling down which legislation must always achieve. The most superficial study of any society, whether from the point of view of wealth, intellect, courage, or quality of any sort or kind, will show that the minority is at the top, the mass are at the bottom, and the levelling process whenever attempted must be performed well below the middle line. Thus, when we legislate for a standard of building, a rate of wage, or uniformity in any practical matter, the line has to be drawn at a level which can be reached by most if not all. That is to say, the line must be very near to the lowest level. After more than thirty years during which this levelling notion has been applied to a large part of the actions of man, its stupidity and its dangers are beginning to be realised. The next generation, in the course of its enquiries into our stewardship of human affairs, will demand to know why we, who inherited the highest standard of living ever known in any land at any time, left our country in the third or fourth place. It is not pleasant to reiterate the horrible suggestion that our children will curse us, but when they find that we who might have kept them on the top of civilisation have put them behind other nations, and have robbed them of the premier position in the march of progress, it will be hard to blame them for looking back upon us without affection or pride. The intolerable conceit which has led us to believe that we can regulate the private affairs of everybody, will be seen by them to have

resulted in the degradation of each class of society
to a lower level. They will with justice accuse us
of distributing among an unworthy generation
the savings of our grandfathers, and of leaving
nothing upon which they can build.

No figure in the Account Rendered can be
estimated to represent the appalling loss which
is caused by the diversion of so much of our effort
and thought to the absurd laws which we have
imposed upon ourselves. In these days it
is of much more importance to know your laws
than to know your trade. Indeed, when we have
exhausted the possibilities of legal phraseology
as a substitute for honesty, some of the modern
law-makers will no doubt be tempted to devise
questionnaires and forms which can be used in
place of hammers and saws and scientific knowledge.

Future generations, able to get our actions into
right perspective, to see the whole picture and
to measure the effect of current tendencies, will
notice that the citizens of the period 1900–30
acted upon the assumption that every one of their
forty-five millions was either a knave or a fool.
They will not distinguish between Socialism and
Conservatism and Liberalism. They will not
bother to enquire which party designed our
bathing-suits or controlled our currency. They
will see quite clearly that we consisted in our own
estimation of two great classes, one actuated
by evil motives and the other devoid of intelligence or usefulness. They will describe a period

of great Parliamentary activity in which companies, firms, business men, financiers, merchants, manufacturers, employers, shopkeepers, salesmen, all the self-supporting workers and all who tried to live by the exercise of their intelligence or skill, were classed as knaves and were surrounded with inspectors and thwarted and hampered at every turn. They will notice that the rest were assumed by Parliament to be entirely without any intelligence, any initiative, any desire to do their bit, or any of the ordinary human qualities of husbands or fathers, and had therefore to be surrounded with further inspectors to hand out doles, nurse their babies, tell them how and when to work, what to do and especially what not to do, and generally to organise and rationalise them into various grades and degrees of demoralising pauperism. When students of these matters further notice that all this was done in the name of progress they may have some doubt as to the knaves – they will be quite certain as to the fools.

Three main motives are traceable behind the actions of the new politics, and are responsible for most of the legislation which worries and muddles and stops us. The first has a sentimental quality, and is in essence good – the desire to relieve poverty. It is an impulse that will remain, but later generations will discover that we applied less wisdom to its satisfaction than we might have done. We did succeed, they will notice, in temporarily improving the lot of a few of the poor, but we did it by means which impoverished the whole and left the future with an ever-growing problem of poverty. The second of the three main motives is not so good. It is the natural desire of the producer to get something more for his product than the buyer is willing to give. Our children will see that in pursuance of this less worthy motive we produced higher wages and higher profits for ever-diminishing numbers of producers in an ever-dwindling market. The third and least worthy of all, though perhaps the most general motive, is natural jealousy of those in better economic positions. This motive, if operating in a sane society, helps to make progress. If jealousy leads anyone to make the effort necessary to reach a higher rung upon the social ladder, the motive may be unworthy, but the economic result is good for all. Our successors will, however, see quite clearly that by allowing this unworthy motive to take too high a place in our thoughts, we did in effect remove the ladder that would otherwise have enabled the jealous to turn their sense of grievance to constructive ends.

The new politics has this extraordinary feature about it, that it ignores the psychology of the governed. We apply our ideas to other people without any regard to their probable effect upon the subject of the experiment. The result is fatal both to the knaves and to the fools. We impose a devastating nervousness upon taxpayers, business men, and labourers – indeed, on all who desire to make any personal effort. This can be illustrated if we consider for a moment a typical case. Imagine in the year 1930 the sort of considerations which pass through the mind of a factory-owner who is contemplating the installation of a new machine. The makers of the machine, as they are bound to do, place its claims high. They explain how it will effect savings in various directions, how its output will be higher, and how the cost of it will certainly be recouped within a given and generally very short period. The manufacturer will receive all this information with due caution. He will know from past experience that hopes such as these do not always materialise, but, balancing in his mind the pros and the cons, he feels inclined to take the risk, make the experiment, and hope for the best. Having, however, got so far, he is faced with a number of other entirely artificial difficulties which are less capable of exact measurement. For example, if he instals the machine, the trade union may intervene and refuse to work it. The factory inspectors may refuse to pass it, not on account of any practical difficulty, but because of some technical incapacity to conform to phraseology which has to apply to any one of the millions of machines in the land. The rate collector will call before the machine is working and will assess it, a process which may mean months of worry, for the assessment will have to be made with the sanction and the approval, after much consultation and argument between them, of local and county and national authorities. The income tax department will take the new machine into consideration, and depreciation, which progresses more rapidly as science advances, must be set almost entirely against profits to be earned. He will find that the new machine complicates his already intricate insurance arrangements. Next, because the new machine, as one of its advantages, occupies less space, it will alter the proportions of his building as between the manufacturing, selling, and accountancy departments, and will reopen all the complications of the derating swindle which in recent years have caused him so much worry. These are a few of the obvious difficulties which arise in a preliminary consideration of the apparently simple question of installing a new machine. They by no means exhaust the catalogue of trouble. All these complications arise, it will be noted, from the mania for Government, the determination of all of us to manage the affairs of everybody else. Not a single one of these difficulties is any part of the practical problem of installing a machine to provide more material comfort for the benefit of society. They are all artificial additions to the necessary work of the world, but in the mind of the factory owner artificial additions assume much larger proportions than the practical work. The most superficial examination of the psychology of the governed must lead us to the view that we pay a very great deal in actual comfort and wealth for the supposed benefits arising from these arrangements.

When the governed is one of the beneficiaries

of the new politics, one of the fools instead of one of the knaves, the psychological effect of all the new arrangements upon him is even more harmful. When, further, he or she is a youth or a maiden without experience of a world which had some touch with the practical work of life, the effect is nothing short of disastrous. Imagine the state of mind of a boy of twenty who was recently the subject of an impassioned address by a well-meaning bishop, completely devoid of economic sense. The boy, the son of a miner, had lived all his life in a mining village. The pits had been closed since he was seventeen. His father was existing on the dole. The boy considered himself a prospective miner, and was hanging about this little village, never having done a day's work in his life, waiting for the condition of society so to change as to enable him to go down the pit in accordance with the union rules, and presumably enjoy a livelihood as a result. The bishop was angry with society for failing to provide this boy with the means of living this particular life. He expressed no anger with the new politics which had produced this tragedy. He ignored the condition of the boy's mind altogether. He failed to see that the boy had not begun to realise the excuse for his existence. He made no complaint that the boy was left in ignorance of his duty, as a member of a civilised community, to render some service which was required by others at a price which others would willingly pay. The boy, according to the bishop, was entitled to sit in a derelict village and wait for society to consume coal, whether coal was wanted or not, at a price agreeable to the boy, whether society could pay it or not, and further to demand, pending the arrival of these conditions, that he, the boy, should be provided with the necessities of life. The worst of the curses which our children will place upon us, and with perfect justice, is that we allowed hundreds of thousands of God-made human beings to remain in complete ignorance of the fact that civilised life is a struggle with the forces of nature, and that each and every one of us has a definite amount of responsibility and a share of that struggle. We are so acting as to lead both knaves and fools to believe that the material needs of life are like manna from heaven, heaven to this generation being a place full of Acts of Parliament. In an address at Ottawa on "Medicine and Statesmanship," Lord Dawson of Penn approached these matters from a slightly different point of view, and I quote from *The Times* summary of his remarks. Having described the rise of preventive medicine and the awakening of medical science to the possibilities of constructive nurture, Lord Dawson said that parallel to these developments, statesmanship, having achieved liberty and equality for the individual, had developed a parental function. "This parental rôle was growing apace. It provided help for those who were born, taught, sick, hungry, thirsty, unemployed. It regulated wages and hours of labour. It was prompted by a social conscience

which inspired man's onward progress. At the
same time it cost the State one quarter of the
national income to maintain these services, which
shepherded us from the cradle to the grave.
There was no attribute of the human being more
notable than his individuality, and the doctor
had ever to take stock of the personal factor.
Was not personality of equal importance to the
statesman? Just as the doctor must realise the
social background, so the statesman must achieve
a just weighing of the rôles of the State and the
individual. Was it possible for the large organisation of the State completely to appreciate the
varying needs of the individual man? Was not
the State compelled to assume a man so stan-
dardised as to be hypothetical rather than real?"

APPENDIX I

NUMBERING OF STATISTICAL TABLES FOR PURPOSES
OF REFERENCE

Heading	*Number*
Gross Liabilities of the State, Estimated Assets, and Exchequer Balances .	IA (Cols. 1–6)
	IB (Cols. 7–12)
Total Amount of Money Issued from the Exchequer or Applied from Other Sources for the Redemption of Debt .	IIA (Cols. 1–6)
Amount Raised by the Creation of Debt, etc.	IIB (Cols. 7–11)
Movement of Exchequer Balance and Estimated Assets	III
Outstanding Loan Debt of Local Authorities of England and Wales .	IVA
Outstanding Loan Debt of the Local Authorities of Scotland and Ireland .	IVB
Detailed Statement of Capital Liabilities in respect of Sums borrowed under various Acts . . .	VA (Cols. 1–5)
	VB (Cols. 6–10)
	VC (Cols. 11–15)
	VD (Cols. 16–19)
Gross and Net Expenditure charged against Public Revenue on Account of the National Debt, and other Payments connected with Capital Liabilities	VIA (Cols. 1–5)
	VIB (Cols. 6–8)

TABLE IA

THE GROSS CAPITAL LIABILITIES OF THE STATE, THE ESTIMATED ASSETS, AND THE EXCHEQUER BALANCES, AT THE CLOSE OF EACH FINANCIAL YEAR

Mar. 31	Nominal Amount of Funded Debt (1) £	Estimated Capital Liability in respect of Terminable Annuities (2) £	Unfunded Debt			Total Dead-weight Debt (Cols. 1–4) (6) £
			Internal Floating (3) £	Other (4) £	Total (5) £	
1914	586,717,872	29,552,219	13,000,000	20,500,000	33,500,000	649,770,091
1920	314,952,215	19,813,709	1,263,683,000	6,230,930,171 *2,965,205	7,494,613,171 *2,965,205	7,828,779,095 *2,965,205
1921	314,836,970	17,698,090	1,243,181,000	5,998,642,426 *11,051,204	7,241,823,426 *11,051,204	7,574,358,486 *11,051,204
1922	580,606,799	16,191,166	1,020,915,500	6,036,587,711 *21,993,933	7,057,503,211 *21,993,933	7,654,301,176 *21,993,933
1923	997,840,225	13,681,065	809,907,500	5,920,804,497 *30,163,221	6,730,711,997 *30,163,221	7,742,233,287 *30,163,221
1924	980,258,479	13,451,342	774,475,500	5,872,861,631 *39,576,401	6,647,337,131 *39,576,401	7,641,046,952 *39,576,401
1925	1,022,689,486	13,053,408	742,195,000	5,819,910,159 *48,523,735	6,562,105,159 *48,523,735	7,597,848,053 *48,523,735
1926	1,073,520,668	12,639,540	704,296,000	5,768,188,191 *57,271,450	6,472,484,191 *57,271,450	7,558,644,299 *57,271,450
1927	1,219,781,953	12,242,000	715,776,000	5,606,817,694 *68,327,905	6,322,593,694 *68,327,905	7,554,617,647 *68,327,905
1928	1,349,963,481	12,551,086	688,790,000	5,476,512,311 *83,111,625	6,165,302,311 *83,111,625	7,527,816,878 *83,111,625
1929	1,478,287,691	12,531,110			6,009,518,853 *95,170,500	7,500,337,654 *95,170,500

*Funding Loan and Victory Bonds to these amounts were tendered for Death Duties, and are therefore included in the columns for Liabilities and for Assets

TABLE I b

THE GROSS CAPITAL LIABILITIES OF THE STATE, THE ESTIMATED ASSETS, AND THE EXCHEQUER BALANCES, AT THE CLOSE OF EACH FINANCIAL YEAR

Mar. 31	Other Capital Liabilities in respect of sums borrowed under various Acts 7	Aggregate Gross Liabilities of the State (Cols. 6 & 7) 8	Estimated Assets			Exchequer Balances at the Banks of England and Ireland 12
			Suez Canal Shares, Estimated market value 9	Other 10	Total 11	
	£	£	£	£	£	£
1914	56,384,019	706,154,110	34,929,000	3,350,578	38,279,578	10,434,519
1920	46,862,866	7,875,641,961 *2,965,205	23,192,000	83,730,187 *2,965,205	106,922,187 *2,965,205	9,369,097
1921	48,738,642	7,623,097,128 *11,051,204	19,364,000	64,705,243 *11,051,204	84,069,243 *11,051,204	3,074,506
1922	66,231,038	7,720,532,214 *21,993,933	19,740,125	93,171,744 *21,993,933	112,911,869 *21,993,933	11,173,530
1923	70,329,238	7,812,562,525 *30,163,221	19,206,335	95,244,054 *30,163,221	114,450,389 *30,163,221	6 818,167
1924	66,490,593	7,707,537,545 *39,576,401	22,416,737	89,243,137 *39,576,401	111,759,874 *39,576,401	6,681,614
1925	68,032,092	7,665,880,145 *48,523,735	35,022,750	80,167,046 *48,523,735	115,189,796 *48,523,735	6,557,100
1926	75,078,203	7,633,722,502 *57,271,450	32,121,885	64,088,836 *57,271,450	96,210,721 *57,271,450	6,556,933
1927	98,070,257	7,652,687,904 *68,327,905	36,194,585	81,502,737 *68,327,905	117,697,322 *68,327,905	6,459,656
1928	103,155,893	7,630,972,670 *83,111,625	51,343,115	80,692,456 *83,111,625	132,035,571 *83,111,625	6,322,625
1929	120,515,893	7,620,853,547 *95,170,500	72,258,844	91,254,371 *95,170,500	163,513,215 *95,170,500	6,252,524

*Funding Loan and Victory Bonds to these amounts were tendered for Death Duties, and are therefore included in the columns for Liabilities and for Assets

TABLE IIA

TOTAL AMOUNT OF MONEY ISSUED FROM THE EXCHEQUER OR APPLIED FROM OTHER SOURCES FOR THE REDEMPTION OF DEBT, IN EACH FINANCIAL YEAR

(Ending March 31)

31 Mar.	Issued from Exchequer				Derived from other sources	TOTAL of Cols. 1–5
	Charged agst. Revenue of year	Old Sinking Fund of Previous year	Taken out of Exchequer Balance or out of the proceeds of fresh loans	Other Issues from Exchequer		
	1	2	3	4	5	6
	£	£	£	£	£	£
1914	10,531,154	180,069	—	712,150	326,311	11,749,684
1920	9,166,581	—	560,679,769	436,313	789,894	571,072,557
1921	25,103,384* 230,556,789*	—	119,757,000	474,790	1,371,719	377,263,682
1922	28,996,983 45,693,246*	—	399,449,050	762,403	873,826	475,775,508
1923	28,978,638* 101,515,848*	—	226,922,353	3,514,710	2,438,265	363,369,814
1924	44,653,644* 48,239,073*	—	82,446,236	7,908,265	2,863,956	186,111,174
1925	49,948,748* 3,658,884	—	104,869,133	6,672,441	6,176,463	171,325,669
1926	54,685,028	—	96,930,758	2,205,141	3,494,419	157,315,346
1927	64,685,087	—	40,294,805	676,703	3,332,826	108,989,421
1928	69,338,629	—	175,134,284	4,992,726	4,130,536	253,596,175
1929	62,176,842	—	200,906,628	1,432,907	780,164	265,296,541

* In these years the Old Sinking Fund was all applied in redeeming debt within the year and under the Finance Acts 1920–4 the amounts so applied were considered as expenditure. They are accordingly shown in Col. 1. Prior to 1922–3 the issue to the Depreciation Fund under the Finance Act 1917 was included in Col. 3. In subsequent years it is charged against the revenue of the year, and is included in the amount shown in Col. 1.

TABLE IIb

AMOUNT RAISED BY THE CREATION OF DEBT TOGETHER WITH OTHER TRANSACTIONS AFFECTING CAPITAL LIABILITIES IN EACH FINANCIAL YEAR

(Ending March 31)

Mar. 31	Money Raised by the Creation of Debt and other Capital Liabilities			TOTAL of Cols. 7–9	NET RESULT. Excess or Defect of Col. 10 over Col. 6.
	By creation of Internal Floating Debt (net)	By the issue of other loans	By creation of other Capital Liabilities		
	7	8	9	10	11
	£	£	£	£	£
1914	3,500,000	—	4,046,249	7,546,249	— 4,203,435
1920	—	917,100,843	4,823,000	921,923,843	+ 350,851,286
1921	—	112,091,669	6,087,000	118,178,669	— 259,085,013
1922	—	417,838,871	21,994,974	439,833,845	— 35,941,663
1923	—	219,621,079	13,277,000	232,898,079	— 130,471,735
1924	—	81,857,997	8,516,500	90,374,497	— 95,826,667
1925	—	99,079,369	13,058,797	112,138,166	— 59,187,503
1926	—	95,248,375	14,152,976	109,401,351	— 47,913,995
1927	13,677,000	62,874,101	28,946,210	105,497,311	— 3,492,110
1928	—	170,573,760	13,540,000	184,113,760	— 69,482,415
1929	51,161,000	153,743,358	22,730,000	227,634,358	— 37,662,183

TABLE III

MOVEMENT (INCREASE OR DECREASE) OF EXCHEQUER BALANCE AND ESTIMATED ASSETS FOR EACH FINANCIAL YEAR   (Ending March 31)

Mar. 31	Increase or Decrease of Exchequer Balance	Increase or Decrease of Estimated Assets	Net Increase or Decrease of Exchequer Balance and Estimated Assets combined
	£	£	£
1914	+ 4,105,359	— 4,443,155	— 337,796
1920	— 3,430,409	+ 22,853,526	+ 19,423,117
1921	— 6,294,591	+ 14,766,945	+ 21,061,536
1922	+ 8,099,024	+ 39,785,355	+ 47,884,379
1923	— 4,355,363	+ 9,707,808	+ 5,352,445
1924	— 186,553	+ 6,722,665	+ 6,536,112
1925	— 74,514	+ 12,377,256	+ 12,302,742
1926	— 167	— 10,231,360	— 10,231,527
1927	— 97,277	+ 32,543,056	+ 32,445,779
1928	— 137,031	+ 29,121,969	+ 28,984,938
1929	— 70,101	+ 31,477,644	+ 31,407,543

TABLE IVa

OUTSTANDING LOAN DEBT OF THE LOCAL AUTHORITIES OF ENGLAND AND WALES

	1913–14 (approx.) £	1922–3 £	1923–4 £	1924–5 £	1925–6 £	1926–7 £
TOTAL	562,630,045	803,880,725	820,262,540	864,882,330	934,656,498	1,027,857,647
The more considerable items are:						
Housing and Town-Planning	12,495,466	191,991,821	199,451,481	219,485,147	260,619,212	319,804,159
Waterworks	131,095,247	143,073,924	144,772,500	148,059,326	152,197,044	155,706,281
Harbours, Docks, Piers, Canals, and Quays	79,602,746	90,240,656	87,938,497	89,372,484	91,334,197	92,795,165
Highways and Bridges	61,703,906	70,270,178	73,580,481	80,025,082	85,468,136	91,858,022
Electricity Supply Undertakings	30,790,851	54,249,963	58,699,552	63,876,009	70,608,032	79,250,025
Sewers and Sewage Disposal	Not Available	44,416,344	46,211,403	49,241,397	52,380,176	55,154,139
Education (Elementary and Higher)	52,113,169	43,829,303	42,589,298	41,920,384	43,260,395	46,039,772
Tramways and Light Railways	37,723,977	37,450,765	36,801,408	37,888,629	38,143,354	39,336,083
Gasworks	22,537,201	24,763,570	24,728,978	25,238,401	25,805,183	27,529,105
Small Holdings and Allotments	4,685,936	19,440,849	19,738,815	19,959,368	20,197,323	20,256,411
THE ABOVE TEN ITEMS THUS ACCOUNTED FOR £928,189,162, OR 90% OF THE TOTAL IN 1926–7						
Standing to the credit of Sinking Funds for the Repayment of Loans	35,701,828	62,415,462	61,822,041	63,108,859	62,800,231	67,825,518

TABLE IVB

THE OUTSTANDING LOAN DEBT OF THE LOCAL AUTHORITIES OF SCOTLAND AND IRELAND

SCOTLAND	1913–14	1920–1	1921–2	1922–3
	£	£	£	£
Outstanding Loans .	63,686,773	67,831,314	84,825,592 (1)	91,500,061
Annuities; capitalised values . .	3,209,671	1,765,190	1,461,132	1,548,497

IRELAND	1913–14	1922–3	1923–4	1924–5
	£	£	£	£
Outstanding Loans .	25,451,911 (2)	11,464,720 (3)	11,537,827 (3)	12,945,912 (3)

THE TOTAL OUTSTANDING LOAN DEBT OF THE LOCAL AUTHORITIES OF THE UNITED KINGDOM IN 1925–6 (TAKING THE LATEST AVAILABLE FIGURES FOR SCOTLAND AND IRELAND) WAS £1,033.9 MLN.

(1) At the close of the year Sinking Funds amounting to £1,318,507 were available for the redemption of certain of these outstanding loans.
(2) All Ireland.
(3) Northern Ireland only.

TABLE Va

DETAILED STATEMENT OF CAPITAL LIABILITIES IN RESPECT OF SUMS BORROWED UNDER VARIOUS ACTS, GIVING LIABILITY CREATED OR REDEEMED DURING, AND THE AMOUNT OUTSTANDING AT THE END OF EACH FINANCIAL YEAR

March 31		Naval Works Acts 1895–1905	Military Works Acts 1897–1903	Telegraph Acts, 1892–1925, and P.O. and Telegraph (Money) Act, 1928	Uganda Railway Acts, 1896–1902	Royal Niger Company Act, 1899
		1	2	3	4	5
		£	£	£	£	£
1920	C.	—	—	2,565,000	—	—
	R.	824,139	565,842	1,232,648	261,361	33,093
	O.	11,285,103	5,607,297	12,759,077	1,734,822	346,282
1921	C.	—	—	5,900,000	—	—
	R.	848,863	582,902	1,264,231	268,921	34,086
	O.	10,436,240	5,024,395	17,394,846	1,465,901	312,196
1922	C.	—	—	7,961,474	—	—
	R.	874,329	600,478	1,371,046	276,700	35,108
	O.	9,561,911	4,423,917	23,985,274	1,189,201	277,088
1923	C.	—	—	7,010,000	—	—
	R.	1,648,158	1,405,284	1,565,559	284,705	36,162
	O.	7,913,753	3,018,633	29,429,715	904,496	240,926
1924	C.	—	—	7,670,000	—	—
	R.	927,576	637,237	1,920,578	292,941	37,247
	O.	6,986,177	2,381,396	35,179,137	611,555	203,679
1925	C.	—	—	9,650,000	—	—
	R.	955,403	656,452	2,045,185	301,417	38,363
	O.	6,030,774	1,724,944	42,783,952	310,138	165,316
1926	C.	—	—	11,950,000	—	—
	R.	403,691	676,250	2,319,288	310,138	39,515
	O.	5,627,083	1,048,694	52,414,664	—	125,801
1927	C.	—	—	11,000,000	—	—
	R.	839,851	1,048,694	2,614,032	—	40,701
	O.	4,787,232	—	60,800,632	—	85,100
1928	C.	—	—	9,900,000	—	—
	R.	428,276	—	3,049,424	—	41,921
	O.	4,358,956	—	67,651,208	—	43,179
1929	C.	—	—	10,550,000	—	—
	R.	441,123	—	3,336,240	—	43,179
	O.	3,917,833	—	74,864,968	—	—

C. =Created   R.=Redeemed   O.= Outstanding

TABLE Vʙ

March 31		Pacific Cable Act, 1901 6	Public Offices (Acquisition of Site) Act, 1895 7	Public Offices (Whitehall) Site Act, 1897 8	Land Registry (New Buildings) Act, 1900 9	Public Buildings' Expenses Act, 1903 10
		£	£	£	£	£
1920	C.	—	—	—	—	—
	R.	39,264	7,430	9,046	5,698	48,543
	O.	1,550,603	332,076	365,130	169,782	1,097,835
1921	C.	—	—	—	—	—
	R.	41,491	7,634	9,296	5,873	50,007
	O.	1,509,112	324,442	355,834	163,909	1,047,828
1922	C.	—	—	—	—	—
	R.	35,759	7,844	9,551	6,054	51,513
	O.	1,473,353	316,598	346,283	157,855	996,315
1923	C.	—	—	—	—	—
	R.	54,180	8,060	9,813	6,240	53,067
	O.	1,419,173	308,538	336,470	151,615	943,248
1924	C.	—	—	—	—	—
	R.	34,970	8,281	10,084	6,432	54,666
	O.	1,384,203	300,257	326,386	145,183	888,582
1925	C.	—	—	—	—	—
	R.	36,019	8,510	10,361	76,456	56,314
	O.	1,348,184	291,747	316,025	68,727	832,268
1926	C.	—	—	—	—	—
	R.	37,099	8,743	10,646	45,683	58,012
	O.	1,311,085	283,004	305,379	23,044	774,256
1927	C.	—	—	—	—	—
	R.	38,212	8,984	10,938	23,044	59,760
	O.	1,272,873	274,020	294,441	—	714,496
1928	C.	—	—	—	—	—
	R.	39,359	9,231	11,239	—	61,562
	O.	1,233,514	264,789	283,202	—	652,934
1929	C.	—	—	—	—	—
	R.	40,539	9,484	11,549	—	63,419
	O.	1,192,975	255,305	271,653	—	589,515

TABLE Vc

March 31		Public Offices Site (Dublin) Act, 1903	Cunard Agreement (Money) Act, 1904	Telephone Transfer Act 1911	Post Office (London) Rly. Act, 1913	Housing Act 1914
		11	12	13	14	15
		£	£	£	£	£
1920	C.	—	—	—	152,000	56,000
	R.	8,394	130,000	563,848	10,558	30,535
	O.	148,582	1,040,000	6,162,228	895,233	1,609,564
1921	C.	—	—	—	144,000	43,000
	R.	8,651	130,000	567,635	13,084	47,553
	O.	139,931	910,000	5,594,593	1,026,149	1,605,011
1922	C.	—	—	—	27,500	56,000
	R.	8,918	130,000	548,041	16,243	32,970
	O.	131,013	780,000	5,046,552	1,037,406	1,628,041
1923	C.	—	—	—	—	27,000
	R.	9,192	130,000	534,773	18,805	35,879
	O.	121,821	650,000	4,511,779	1,018,601	1,619,162
1924	C.	—	—	—	10,500	16,000
	R.	9,474	130,000	572,641	19,944	38,310
	O.	112,347	520,000	3,939,138	1,009,157	1,596,852
1925	C.	—	—	—	—	6,000
	R.	9,766	130,000	587,653	22,628	46,227
	O.	102,581	390,000	3,351,485	986,529	1,556,625
1926	C.	—	—	—	—	6,000
	R.	10,066	130,000	552,217	24,743	408,065
	O.	92,515	260,000	2,799,268	961,786	1,154,560
1927	C.	—	—	—	—	6,000
	R.	10,376	130,000	524,941	26,086	30,917
	O.	82,139	130,000	2,274,327	935,700	1,123,643
1928	C.	—	—	—	—	—
	R.	10,695	130,000	608,537	27,424	34,472
	O.	71,444		1,665,790	908,276	1,089,171
1929	C.	—	—	—	—	—
	R.	11,023	—	568,712	28,829	34,222
	O.	60,421	—	1,097,078	879,447	1,054,949

TABLE Vᴅ

March 31		Anglo-Persian Oil Co. Acquisition of Capital Acts, 1914 & 1919 ; and Payment of Calls Act, 1922 — 16	Unemployment Insurance Acts 1921 — 17	West Indian Islands (Telegraph) Act, 1924 — 18	Total of Cols. 1–18 — 19
		£	£	£	£
1920	C.	2,050,000	—	—	4,823,000
	R.	290,748	—	—	4,061,147
	O.	1,759,252	—	—	46,862,866
1921	C.	—	—	—	6,087,000
	R.	330,997	—	—	4,211,224
	O.	1,428,255	—	—	48,738,642
1922	C.	—	13,950,000	—	21,994,974
	R.	498,024	—	—	4,502,578
	O.	930,231	13,950,000	—	66,231,038
1923	C.	950,000	5,290,000	—	13,277,000
	R.	978,923	2,400,000	—	9,178,800
	O.	901,308	16,840,000	—	70,329,238
1924	C.	—	820,000	—	8,516,500
	R.	444,764	7,210,000	—	12,355,145
	O.	456,544	10,450,000	—	66,490,593
1925	C.	—	3,060,000	342,797	13,058,797
	R.	456,544	6,080,000	—	11,517,298
	O.	—	7,430,000	342,797	68,032,092
1926	C.	—	2,150,000	46,976	14,152,976
	R.	—	2,070,000	2,709	7,106,865
	O.	—	7,510,000	387,064	75,078,203
1927	C.	—	17,942,431	3,779	28,946,210
	R.	—	542,000	5,620	5,954,156
	O.	—	24,910,431	385,223	98,070,257
1928	C.	—	3,640,000	—	13,540,000
	R.	—	3,996,000	6,325	8,454,465
	O.	—	24,554,431	378,898	103,155,792
1929	C.	—	12,180,000	—	22,730,000
	R.	—	774,431	7,149	5,369,899
	O.	—	35,960,000	371,749	120,515,893

TABLE VIa

GROSS AND NET EXPENDITURE CHARGED AGAINST PUBLIC REVENUE ON ACCOUNT OF THE NATIONAL DEBT, AND OTHER PAYMENTS CONNECTED WITH CAPITAL LIABILITIES IN EACH FINANCIAL YEAR (ending March 31).

Mar. 31	Issues on account of INTEREST AND MANAGEMENT £ 1	Issues on account of CAPITAL (Including New Sinking Fund) £ 2	TOTAL ISSUES £ 3	Sundry Receipts to be set off	
				Against the Issues on account of Interest and Management £ 4	Against the Issues on account of Capital £ 5
1914	18,704,132	10,531,154	29,235,286	299,376	—
1920	328,174,370	9,166,581	337,340,951	692,506	—
1921	329,895,122	255,660,173	585,555,295	1,062,885	526
1922	309,220,505	74,690,229	383,910,734	2,617,224	—
1923	302,247,486	130,494,486	432,741,972	2,419,491	—
1924	310,453,537	92,982,717	403,436,254	2,642,528	—
1925	315,120,546	53,607,632	368,728,178	2,538,376	62,142
1926	311,397,548	54,685,028	366,082,576	2,551,540	103,276
1927	322,484,612	64,685,087	387,169,699	4,063,830	82,448
1928	318,621,119	69,338,629	387,959,748	4,765,876	27,587
1929	315,414,907	62,176,842	377,591,749	5,037,356	20,775

TABLE VIb

| Mar. 31 | Net Expenditure | | Total of Cols. 6 and 7 |
	Representing INTEREST AND MANAGEMENT 6	Representing PAYMENT OF CAPITAL 7	8
1914	£ 18,404,756	£ 10,531,154	£ 28,935,910
1920	327,481,864	9,166,581	336,648,445
1921	328,832,237	255,659,647	584,491,884
1922	306,603,281	74,690,229	381,293,510
1923	299,827,995	130,494,486	430,322,481
1924	307,811,009	92,982,717	400,793,726
1925	312,582,170	53,545,490	366,127,660
1926	308,846,008	54,581,752	363,427,760
1927	318,420,782	64,602,639	383,023,421
1928	313,855,243	69,317,042	383,172,285
1929	310,377,549	62,156,067	372,533,616

APPENDIX II

DETAILS OF FUNDED, UNFUNDED, AND EXTERNAL DEBT, AND ESTIMATED ASSETS

DETAILS OF FUNDED DEBT

	March 31, 1926			March 31, 1927			March 31, 1928			March 31, 1929		
	£	s.	d.	£	s.	d.	£	s.	d.	£	s.	d.
2½% Consols	276,329,287	5	10	276,296,164	0	7	276,243,161	19	5	276,225,754	16	7
2¾% Annuities	2,399,679	5	10	2,399,679	5	10	2,399,679	5	10	2,399,679	5	10
2½% Annuities	21,130,356	17	8	21,120,356	17	8	21,120,356	17	8	21,120,356	17	8
3½% Conversion Loan	760,015,375	13	5	739,935,758	9	6	832,257,624	15	7	811,033,966	14	1
4% Consols				166,384,124	17	2	204,296,789	6	2	353,862,063	19	2
Debts to the Banks of England and Ireland, 2¼%	13,645,869	4	8	13,645,869	4	8	13,645,869	4	8	13,645,869	4	8
TOTAL FUNDED DEBT	1,073,520,568	7	5	1,219,781,952	15	5	1,349,963,481	9	4	1,478,287,690	18	0

TERMINABLE ANNUITIES

	March 31, 1926			March 31, 1927			March 31, 1928			March 31, 1929		
	£	s.	d.	£	s.	d.	£	s.	d.	£	s.	d.
Estimated capital liability in respect of Annuities for Life and Terms of Years	12,639,540	0	0	12,242,000	0	0	12,551,086	0	0	12,551,110	0	0

DETAILS OF THE UNFUNDED DEBT

	March 31, 1926	March 31, 1927	March 31, 1928	March 31, 1929
	£	£	£	£
Treasury Bills	564,855,000	599,175,000	526,940,000	700,295,000
Ways and Means Advances	139,441,000	116,601,000	161,850,000	37,050,000
3½% War Loan (1925–28)	62,713,997	62,713,997	—	—
4½% War Loan (1925–45)	12,804,441	12,804,441	12,804,341	12,804,341
4% War Loan (1929–42)	64,914,955	65,968,081	80,334,321	79,684,835
5% War Loan (1927–47)	2,044,052,511	2,088,173,683	2,172,273,230	2,184,468,777
4% Funding Loan (1960–90)	391,909,485	388,777,644	385,387,613	382,059,454
4% Victory Bonds	347,609,045	345,334,645	342,968,645	340,509,945
4½% Conversion Loan (1940–44)	210,586,966	211,106,932	220,948,841	223,119,139
3% Exchequer Bonds (28 Jan 1930)	15,640,000	15,640,000	15,640,000	15,640,000
5½% Treasury Bonds (1 April 1929)	30,637,387	30,637,382	30,637,382	30,168,186
5½% Treasury Bonds (15 May 1930)	134,741,018	134,741,018	134,741,018	134,741,018
5% Treasury Bonds (1 February 1927)	109,631,887	—	—	—
4½% Treasury Bonds (15 April 1932)	121,265,764	121,265,764	121,265,764	121,265,764
4% Treasury Bonds (1931–33)	60,853,000	64,585,000	64,585,000	64,585,000
4½% Treasury Bonds (1934)	19,192,873	99,607,061	91,773,523	77,202,405
5% Treasury Bonds (1933–35)	—	—	159,535,295	114,607,893
4½% Treasury Bonds (1932–34)	—	—	—	123,453,319
4½% Treasury Bonds Annual (Due Feb. 1 following year)	5,109,643	3,403,036	72,853,528	14,571,118
5% National War Bonds (1 Oct. 1927)	158,116,141	69,917,461	—	—
4% National War Bonds (1 Oct. 1927)	79,983,254	41,907,949	—	—
5% National War Bonds (1 April 1928)	122,283,334	110,081,063	26,264,087	—
4% National War Bonds (1 April 1928)	37,385,098	36,430,477	19,568,442	—
5% National War Bonds (1 Sept. 1928)	189,820,025	177,935,322	41,952,209	—
4% National War Bonds (1 Sept. 1928)	20,612,713	20,269,956	6,102,899	—
5% National War Bonds (1 Feb. 1929)	92,690,565	93,930,719	95,160,661	—
4% National War Bonds (1 Feb. 1929)	4,808,665	4,799,565	—	—
National Savings Certificates	375,575,390	371,823,328	362,447,780	361,238,312
National Saving Bonds	—	84,346	617,777	787,538
OTHER DEBT created under the War Loan Acts 1914–1919:				
5% Loan from Straits Settlements (1934)	1,753,000	1,753,000	1,753,000	1,753,000
Loans from individuals without interest	250	150	50	50
TOTAL INTERNAL UNFUNDED DEBT	5,418,987,308	5,289,467,999	5,153,184,473	5,020,005,095

DETAILS OF EXTERNAL DEBT

	March 31, 1926	March 31, 1927	March 31, 1928	March 31, 1929
	£	£	£	£
Debt created under the War Loan Acts 1914–1919 :				
United States of America :				
Government Loan	930,821,918	995,684,932	920,547,945	915,000,000
5¼% 10-Year Bonds (1929)	4,001,199	2,905,644	1,819,110	412,850
5½% 20-Year Bonds (1937)	29,504,178	29,504,178	29,503,562	29,503,562
6% Central Argentine Railway Co. (1927)	3,082,192	—	—	—
Straits Settlements :				
5¼% Loan 1928	3,341,000	3,341,000	3,341,000	—
5% Loan 1929	4,315,000	4,315,000	4,315,000	4,315,000
Loans from Allied Governments :				
France (a)	53,500,000	53,500,000	53,500,000	53,500,000
Russia (a)	60,000,000	60,000,000	60,000,000	60,000,000
Italy (a)	22,200,000	22,200,000	22,200,000	21,950,000
American Loan $13,850 Converted Bonds at 4½%. Sterling equivalent at par	2,846	2,846	2,846	2,846
TOTAL EXTERNAL DEBT	1,110,768,333	1,101,453,600	1,095,229,463	1,084,684,258

(a) These sums may be regarded as available to be set off against debts owed by the same Governments to this country.

DETAILS OF ESTIMATED ASSETS

	March 31, 1926	March 31, 1927	March 31, 1928	March 31, 1929
	£	£	£	£
Estimated Market Value of Suez Canal Shares	32,121,885	36,194,585	51,343,115	72,258,844
Advances for purchase of Bullion for Coinage	400,000	300,000	300,000	300,000
Advances to Unemployment Fund	7,510,000	24,910,431	24,554,431	35,960,000
Contributions of Colonies to Capital Expenditure on Pacific Cable and West India Cable	1,216,220	1,202,642	1,166,715	1,139,511
Nominal Value of Debenture Stock of Cunard Steamship Co. held as security for repayment of advances	260,000	130,000	—	—
Anglo-Persian Oil Co.—Shares and Debenture Stock at Cost	5,200,000	5,200,000	5,200,000	5,200,000
French 4% Rentes at Cost	3,604,306	3,604,306	3,604,306	3,604,306
Rumanian 4% Consolidation Bonds			1,890,000	1,910,000
India—Outstanding Liability in respect of 5% War Loan	18,320,805	17,807,802	17,276,173	16,721,003
Isle of Man	217,745	608,559	588,922	568,505
Depreciation Fund—Balance applicable to Debt Reduction	8,919,377	9,064,354	8,949,742	9,078,691
Land Settlement Acts Loans outstanding	15,272,227	15,031,217	14,845,225	14,672,932
Victory Bonds Sinking Fund—Balance applicable to Debt Reduction	1,138,108	1,188,768	1,230,635	1,281,297
Funding Loan Sinking Fund—Balance etc.	229,368	310,023	249,141	285,121
3½% War Loan held for Sinking Fund for Telephone Exchequer Bonds	302,635	302,635	—	—
4% Consols Sinking Fund—Balance				59,003
3% Exchequer Bonds, 1930, held for Sinking Fund for Telephone Exchequer Bonds			416,000	469,000
New Sinking Fund 1923—Balance for 4% Consols Sinking Fund	1,498,045			
New Sinking Fund 1928—Balance			3,472	4,316
New Sinking Fund 1923—Balance				
Death Duties—Surrendered Securities Account			417,694	686
TOTAL ESTIMATED ASSETS	96,210,721	115,860,322	132,035,571	163,513,215

Or

APPENDIX III

THE CAPITAL ACCOUNT OF THE STATE

FUNDED DEBT.

1929 Figure
£   s.   d.

1. UNITED KINGDOM 2½% CONSOLS.
   £682,311,359 issued. Redeemable on and after April 5, 1923 in such order and manner as Parliament shall direct at par.
   Created under the National Debt (Conversion) Act, 1888.
   £60,000,000 were issued in April 1901; and £32,000,000 in April 1902.
   £219,426,745 were converted into 4½% War Loan of 1915.
   (*See* Appendix I) 276,225,754 16 7

2. UNITED KINGDOM 2¾% ANNUITIES.
   Issued, £3,735,514. Repayable at par on and after 1905.
   Created under National Debt (Conversion of Stock) Act, 1884.
   £1,045,835 were converted into 4½% War Loan of 1915.
   (*See* Appendix I) 2,399,679 5 10

3. UNITED KINGDOM 2½% ANNUITIES.
   Issued, £29,640,139. Repayable at par on or after 1905; not less than £14,000,000 to be redeemed at one time.
   Originally created, 1853.
   £8,093,266 was converted into 4½% War Loan of 1915.
   (*See* Appendix I) 21,120,356 17 8

4. UNITED KINGDOM 3½% CONVERSION LOAN OF 1921.
   Issued, £930,325,000. Repayable at par on and after April 1st, 1961.
   Issued £689,031,000 in April, 1921, in exchange for 5% National War Bonds, due September 1st, 1925.
   A further £59,660,000 issued for cash in January 1925, to finance payment of maturing debt.
   A further £30,000,000 issued for cash in April 1925, to finance payment of 5–15 year Treasury Bonds, due May 1st, 1925.
   A further £40,000,000 issued for cash in September 1925.

FUNDED DEBT (*contd.*)

    UNITED KINGDOM 3½% CONVERSION LOAN OF 1921 (*contd.*).

	1929 Figure		
	£	s.	d.

A further £111,656,000 issued in September 1927, in conversion for 3½% War Loan, due March 1st, 1928; 5% National War Bonds, due April 1st, 1928; and 4% National War Bonds, due April 1st, 1928.

    (*See* Appendix I)   811,033,966   14   1

5. UNITED KINGDOM 4% CONSOLIDATED LOAN 1927–57.

Issued, £213,979,376. Not redeemable until February 1st, 1957; on and after that date it is redeemable at par on any interest date at the option of the Government.

Offered for public subscription in January 1927, at 85

Offered also for conversion of 5% Treasury Bonds, due February 1st, 1927; 5% National War Bonds, due October 1st, 1927; and 4% National War Bonds, due October 1st, 1927.

    (*See* Appendix I)   353,862,063   19   2

6. Debts to the Banks of England and Ireland (2½%)   13,645,869   4   8

    TOTAL FUNDED DEBT . . .   1,478,287,690   18   0

TERMINABLE ANNUITIES.

These are purchased under various Acts from the National Debt Commissioners in the lifetime of the investor.

The estimated capital liability with regard to them amounted on March 31st, 1929, to .   12,531,110   0   0

UNFUNDED DEBT.

    (Appendix II gives the figures for March 31st, 1926, 1927, 1928, 1929)

1. TREASURY BILLS.

These are bills of exchange issued by the Government as a form of temporary borrowing. They must be repaid by the end of the year and thus make no difference to the amount of the debt at the end of the year, compared with the year before . . .   700,295,000   0   0

2. WAYS AND MEANS ADVANCES . .   37,050,000   0   0

3. 3½% WAR LOAN.

Issued, £350,000,000. Redeemable on and after 1925. Due, 1928.

4. UNITED KINGDOM 4½% WAR LOAN OF 1915.

Issued, £900,357,691. Redeemable at par and interest on and after December 1st, 1925. Due, December 1st, 1945.

£289,797,721 was issued for conversion of Consols, 2¾% and 2½% Annuities and 3½% War Loan.

UNFUNDED DEBT (*contd.*)	1929 Figure		
UNITED KINGDOM 4½% WAR LOAN OF 1915 (*contd.*).	£	*s.*	*d.*
£779,334,588 was converted into 5% and 4% War Loan during financial years 1916–18	12,804,341	9	2
5. UNITED KINGDOM 4% WAR LOAN OF 1917 Issued, £68,109,398. Redeemable at par on and after October 15th, 1929. Due, October 15th, 1942	79,684,834	13	11
6. UNITED KINGDOM 5% WAR LOAN OF 1917. Issued, £2,201,676,166. Redeemable at par on and after June 1st, 1929. Due, June 1st, 1947. An offer of conversion into 4½% War Loan, 1940–44, was made to holders in April 1924, and £148,592,586 of 5% War Loan was so converted	2,184,468,777	7	0
7. UNITED KINGDOM 4% FUNDING LOAN OF 1919 (*a*). Issued, £469,111,000. Redeemable at par on and after May 1st, 1960, at option of the Government. Due, May 1st, 1990 . .	382,059,454	8	11
8. UNITED KINGDOM VICTORY BONDS (4%) OF 1919 (*a*) Issued, £359,531,845. Redeemable, by 1976, at par by annual drawings, beginning September 1st, 1920	340,509,945	0	0
9. UNITED KINGDOM 4½% CONVERSION LOAN OF 1924. Issued, £211,106,932. Due, July 1st, 1944. Redeemable at par at the option of the Government on any interest date on and after July 1st, 1940, upon three months notice	223,119,138	14	4
10. UNITED KINGDOM 3% EXCHEQUER BONDS OF 1918. Issued, £15,640,000. Due, January 28th, 1930. These bonds were issued in exchange for a like amount of Russian Government Sterling Treasury bills, which became due in London on January 28th, 1928	15,640,000	0	0
11. UNITED KINGDOM 5½% TREASURY BONDS, 1921–29. Issued, £245,159,736. Repayable at par on April 1st, 1929. £214,457,000 were converted into 3½% Conversion Loan during the financial year 1922–23	30,168,185	19	8

(*a*) These Bonds may be tendered for Death Duties to be held by the National Debt Commissioners, until drawn or paid off.

UNFUNDED DEBT (*contd.*)

12. UNITED KINGDOM 5½% TREASURY BONDS,
1921–30.
Issued, £134,741,018. Due, May 15th, 1930.
Not redeemable before maturity. Not con-
vertible into any other issue .   .   .   134,741,018   0   0

13. UNITED KINGDOM 4½% TREASURY BONDS,
1932.
Issued, £121,266,764 during 1922. Due,
April 15th, 1932.
Holders of 5% National War Bonds, due
October 1st, 1922 and April 1st, 1923, were
offered conversion into these 4½% Bonds;
those not converted were paid at maturity   121,265,763 16   6

14. UNITED KINGDOM 4% TREASURY BONDS,
1931–33.
Issued, £64,585,000. Dated, April 1st, 1923.
Due, April 15th, 1933. Redeemable as a
whole at the option of the Government at
par, at any time on or after April 15th, 1931   64,585,000   0   0

15. UNITED KINGDOM 4½% TREASURY BONDS,
1929–34.
Issued, £174,473,000. Dated, February 1st,
1927. Due, February 1st, 1934, or on February 1st in each of the years 1929 to 1933
inclusive, at the option of the Government
or of the holders of the Bonds.
First issue, £82,700,000 in October 1926,
offered only for conversion of 5% Treasury
Bonds. Maturing, February 1st, 1927.
Holders of £72,833,528 of the first issue,
required payment on February 1st, 1929.
Second issue, £91,773,000, in September
1927 for cash   77,202,405   0 11

16. UNITED KINGDOM 5% TREASURY BONDS,
1933–35.
Issued, £159,535,000. Dated, January 1928.
Due, February 1st, 1935. Redeemable on or
after February 1st, 1933, at the option of
the Government, at par.
Offered December 1927 and January 1928
for cash, and for conversion of 5% National
War Bonds, due September 1st, 1928, and
of 4% National War Bonds, due Septem-
ber 1st, 1928 .   .   .   .   .   .   114,607,892 16 10

17. UNITED KINGDOM 4½% TREASURY BONDS,
1932–34.
Issued in exchange for National War Bonds
and 4½% Treasury Bonds, 1929 .   .   123,453,319   0   3

UNFUNDED DEBT (*contd.*)

	1929 Figure £	s.	d.
18. UNITED KINGDOM 5% AND 4% NATIONAL WAR BONDS. Issued in four series from October 1917 to May 1929, 5% Bonds are convertible within 14 days after any interest date into 5% War Loan, 1929–47. 4% Bonds are convertible in like manner into 4% War Loan, 1929–42.			
19. NATIONAL SAVINGS CERTIFICATES. First issued as War Savings Certificates during the financial year 1915–16. Continued as National Savings Certificates, 1920–21	361,238,312	0	0
20. NATIONAL SAVING BONDS. Issued 1927 and in subsequent years, for conversion of National Savings Certificates falling due	787,538	2	10
21. OTHER DEBT, created under the War Loan Acts 1914–19. Payable in Sterling:			
5% Loan from the Straits Settlements, 1934	1,753,000	0	0
Loans from individuals without interest .	50	0	0
TOTAL INTERNAL UNFUNDED DEBT .	5,020,005,094	19	6
OTHER DEBT, created under the War Loan Acts, 1914–19. PAYABLE ABROAD: United States of America:			
Government Loan	915,000,000	0	0
5½% 10 Year Bonds, 1929 . . .	412,850	0	0
5½% 20 Year Bonds, 1937 . .	29,503,562	0	0
Straits Settlements: 5% Loan, 1929	4,315,000	0	0
Loans from Allied Governments:			
France	53,500,000	0	0
Russia	60,000,000	0	0
Italy	21,950,000	0	0
American Loan, $13,850 Converted Bonds at 4½%, repayable October 15th, 1930–40. Sterling equivalent at par of exchange .	2,846	0	0
TOTAL EXTERNAL DEBT	1,084,684,258	0	0
TOTAL DEBT	7,595,508,153	17	6
OTHER CAPITAL LIABILITIES, in respect of sums borrowed under various Acts. (For details, *see* Table VA, B, C, D) . .	120,515,893	0	0
TOTAL GROSS CAPITAL LIABILITIES OF THE STATE	7,716,024,046	17	6
Less Funding Loan and Victory Bonds tendered for Death Duties, and held by the National Debt Commissioners until drawn or paid off	95,170,500	6	7
	7,620,853,546	10	11

APPENDIX IV

AGRICULTURAL MARKETING BILL

EXPLANATORY AND FINANCIAL MEMORANDUM

Agricultural Marketing Schemes

The clauses of the Bill grouped under this heading (together with the first three Schedules) propose to allow producers of an agricultural product, to which the Bill applies, to regulate the marketing of that product by means of boards elected by themselves and in accordance with schemes submitted by themselves. It is proposed that such regulation should be confined to products produced in the area to which the scheme is applicable (which may be Great Britain or any part thereof); and the scheme will be binding on all producers of the regulated product in that area. The powers of regulation are set out in clauses 3 to 5.

The interest of the public and of individual producers is protected by requiring the Minister, before approving a scheme, to give notice of it and consider any representations made, and further by giving Parliament the opportunity of resolving that the scheme shall not come into force. The interests of producers are further protected by provisions for independent arbitration and either for exemption from the scheme or for representation on the board administering it. The interest of the general public is further protected by the establishment of a special "Consumers' Committee" for every scheme, whose duty it will be to watch, and consider complaints as to, the effect of the scheme on consumers. The Bill also establishes a "Committee of Investigation" to which the Minister may refer a complaint from a Consumers' Committee or a complaint which would not fall to be considered by a Consumers' Committee. If the Committee of Investigation report that any matter requires rectification, the Minister has power to amend or revoke the scheme, and if necessary to replace the board administering it by persons nominated by him. The Minister is also empowered on his own initiative to lay before Parliament the draft of an order revoking or amending a scheme, such order to come into force unless Parliament resolves to the contrary.

A scheme may also provide for the encouragement of agricultural research and education and may empower a board to make advances to producers.

Agricultural Marketing Funds

The clauses grouped under this heading propose that, for the purpose of financing boards administering the schemes, there shall be paid, out of moneys provided by Parliament, into an English Fund sums not exceeding £500,000 and into a Scottish Fund sums not exceeding £125,000. Out of these Funds a short term loan may be made to a board, when it is first set up, free of interest for two years, but must be repaid within that period unless renewed; a long term loan may be made to a board at any time for any period, but the amount of the Fund that may be immobilised in such loans is limited. Loans may only be made on the recommendation of a special committee appointed under the Bill.

Supplementary

The clauses grouped under this heading contain a provision (clause 13) that any expenses incurred by the Minister in connection with a committee appointed under the Bill shall be defrayed out of moneys provided by Parliament. The aggregate expenses incurred under this provision and of any additional staff which may be required by the Bill are not expected to exceed £20,000 per annum. These clauses also include an interpretation clause and special provisions for Scotland, and, together with the Fourth Schedule, define the products to which the Act applies.

AGRICULTURAL MARKETING BILL

ARRANGEMENT OF CLAUSES

Agricultural Marketing Schemes

Agricultural Marketing Funds

Supplementary

A
BILL

TO

A.D. 1930. Enable schemes to be made for regulating the marketing of certain agricultural products by the producers thereof and for encouraging agricultural research and education, and to provide for purposes connected with the matters aforesaid.

BE it enacted by the King's most Excellent Majesty, by and with the advice and consent of the Lords Spiritual and Temporal, and Commons, in this present Parliament assembled, and by the authority of the same, as follows: —

Agricultural Marketing Schemes

Submission and approval of schemes.

1. — (1) A scheme for any area, regulating the marketing of an agricultural product by the producers thereof, being a product to which this Act applies, may be submitted to the Minister by the persons specified in Part I of the First Schedule to this Act, and the Minister may, subject to the provisions of Part II of that Schedule and to the approval of Parliament, make an order approving the scheme, and any scheme so approved shall, until revoked, have effect as if enacted in this Act.

(2) A scheme may be amended or revoked in accordance with the provisions of Part III of the said Schedule.

(3) Nothing in any scheme shall apply to any product, in so far as it is produced outside the area to which the scheme is applicable.

2.—(1) Every scheme shall provide for the registration of any producer who makes application for that purpose, and shall constitute a board to administer the scheme, which shall be composed of representatives of registered producers elected by them in such manner as may be provided by the scheme:

A.D. 1930.

Constitution of boards to administer schemes.

Provided that, during such period (not being longer than twelve months after the scheme comes into force) as may be specified in the scheme, the board shall be composed of persons nominated by the Minister after consultation with the persons who submitted the scheme.

(2) The provisions of the Second Schedule to this Act shall apply with respect to the incorporation, registration and winding up of any such board.

3. Subject to the approval of the Minister, a scheme may provide for all or any of the following matters, that is to say—

Regulation of marketing and encouragement of education and research.

(*a*) for empowering the board to buy, sell, grade, pack, store, adapt for sale, insure, advertise or transport the regulated product, to manufacture any article from that product and to sell any article so manufactured;

(*b*) for requiring registered producers to sell the regulated product or any kind, variety or grade thereof, only to, or through the agency of, the board;

(*c*) for empowering the board to regulate sales of the regulated product by any registered producer by determining—

(i) the kind, variety or grade of the product which may be sold;

(ii) the quantity of the product or

A.D. 1930.

of any kind, variety or grade thereof which may be sold;

(iii) the price at, below or above which, and the terms on which, the product or any kind, variety, grade or quantity thereof may be sold;

(iv) the persons to, or through the agency of, whom the product or any kind, variety, grade or quantity thereof may be sold;

(*d*) for regulating the manner in which the regulated product is to be graded, packed, stored, adapted for sale, insured, advertised or transported by or on behalf of registered producers;

(*e*) for such matters as are incidental to, or consequential on, the provisions of this Act relating to the contents of schemes or to be necessary for giving effect to those provisions or for enabling the board to encourage agricultural education and research.

Miscellaneous provisions of schemes.

4. Every scheme shall provide for the following matters, that is to say —

(*a*) for requiring that no sale of the regulated product shall be made by any producer who is not either a registered producer or a person exempted from registration by or under the provisions of the scheme;

(*b*) for exempting from all or any of the provisions of the scheme producers of such classes or descriptions as may be specified in the scheme or determined by the board;

(*c*) for requiring the board to impose on, and recover from, any producer who contravenes the scheme such monetary

penalties as may be specified by the A.D. 1930.
scheme;

(*d*) for securing that any producer who is
aggrieved by any act or omission of the
board may refer the matter to one or
more arbitrators appointed in such
manner as may be provided by the
scheme, and for the manner in which any
such reference is to be heard and determined;

(*e*) for the additional matters set out in the
Third Schedule to this Act.

5.—(1) Every scheme shall provide for the Financial
following matters, that is to say:— powers and
duties of
(*a*) for the establishment of a fund (hereafter boards.
in this section referred to as "the fund")
to be administered and controlled by the
board, for the payment into the fund of
all moneys received by the board, and
for the payment out of the fund of any
moneys required by the board for the
operation of the scheme;

(*b*) for enabling the board to recover from
every registered producer contributions
to the fund of such amounts as may be
necessary for the operation of the scheme,
and for the assessment of the contributions of each producer in such manner as
may be provided by the scheme;

(*c*) for requiring the board to pay out of the
fund such sums by way of compensation
as may be necessary for securing that the
provisions of the scheme operate equit-
ably as between all registered producers,
and for the distribution to registered producers, in proportion to their respective

A.D. 1930.

contributions to the fund, of all moneys standing to the credit of the fund which are not required for the operation of the scheme;

(*d*) for empowering the board to borrow money for the purpose of exercising their functions under the scheme.

(2) Any scheme may empower the board to lend to any registered producer sums not exceeding the amount which the board estimate that he will receive from the sale of any quantity of the regulated product produced or in course of production by him.

(3) A debenture issued by the board may create in favour of a bank a floating charge on any farming stock in England the property in which is vested in the board, and any such charge shall be registered in like manner as an agricultural charge under Part II of the Agricultural Credits Act, 1928, and section nine of that Act shall apply to such a charge in like manner as it applies to an agricultural charge, and the charge, if so registered, shall, as respects such property, be valid notwithstanding anything in the Bills of Sale Acts, 1878 and 1882, and shall not be deemed to be a bill of sale within the meaning of those Acts.

18 & 19
Geo. 5. c. 43.

In this subsection the expressions "bank" and "farming stock" have the same meanings respectively as in Part II of the Agricultural Credits Act, 1928.

Effect of
schemes on
contracts.

6. — (1) Subject as hereinafter provided, a contract of which neither the making nor the performance was, at the time when the contract was made, prohibited by or under any scheme in force under this Act, shall not, unless the terms of the contract otherwise provide, be void or unenforceable by reason that, at the time for the performance of any provision of the contract, the performance thereof is so prohibited:

Provided that, where the performance of any contract, made during the period beginning six months before and ending six months after the coming into force of any scheme, is prohibited by or under that scheme, the foregoing provision shall cease to apply to that contract upon the expiration of three months after the prohibition first takes effect, unless the contract is registered under this section.

(2) It shall be the duty of the board, on the application of any party to a contract, to register the contract within the period of fourteen days after the application, unless the board are of opinion that the contract was made with a view to evading the provisions of the scheme and if any party to a contract is aggrieved by the omission of a board to register the contract within the period aforesaid he may, within fourteen days after the expiration of that period, appeal to the Court, and, pending the determination of any such appeal, subsection (1) of this section shall, notwithstanding anything in the proviso thereto, continue to apply to the contract.

(3) On any appeal under this section, the board concerned and any party to the contract may appear and be heard, and if, on the hearing of any such appeal, the contract is found by the Court not to have been made with a view to evading the provisions of the scheme, the Court shall by order direct the registration thereof, and thereupon the contract shall be deemed to have been registered as from the date of the order; but, where the Court does not direct the registration of a contract, any party to the contract certified

Agricultural Marketing. [20 & 21 GEO. 5.]

A.D. 1930.

by the Court to have entered into the contract bona fide without a view to the evasion of the provisions of the scheme may recover the amount of any damage suffered by him by reason of the avoidance of the contract from any party certified by the Court to have entered into the contract with a view to such evasion as aforesaid.

(4) For the purposes of an appeal under this section with respect to any contract, the Court shall be any county court within the district of which any party to the contract has dwelt or carried on business at any time during the period within which the appeal may be brought:

Provided that—

(*a*) if, before proceedings in respect of any such appeal are commenced in the county court, the board and all parties to the contract agree that the appeal should be heard by the High Court, the High Court shall be the Court for the purposes of the appeal; and

51 & 52 Vict.
c. 43.

(*b*) section one hundred and twenty-six of the County Courts Act, 1888 (which provides for the removal of matters from the county court to the High Court), shall apply with respect to any appeal under this section as if the appeal were a matter commenced in the county court under that Act.

(5) No person shall be liable to any penalty in respect of a contravention of any scheme in force under this Act, if he proves that the contravention was necessary for the performance of a contract which, by reason of the foregoing provisions of this section, was not, at the time of the contravention, void or unenforceable.

7.—(1) The Minister shall, immediately after any scheme approved by him comes into force, appoint a committee (hereafter in this section referred to as "a consumers' committee"), which shall be charged with the duty of considering, and reporting to the Minister on the effect of the scheme, and any complaints made as to the effect of the scheme, on consumers of the regulated product.

Every consumers' committee shall consist of a chairman and of not less than six other members, who shall be such persons as appear to the Minister, after consultation with the Board of Trade, to represent the interests of such consumers as aforesaid.

(2) The Minister shall, immediately after the scheme first approved by him comes into force, appoint a committee (hereafter in this section referred to as "the committee of investigation") consisting of a chairman and four other members, which shall be charged with the duty, if the Minister in any case so directs, of considering, and reporting to the Minister on, any report made by a consumers' committee and any complaint made by a consumers' committee and any complaint made to the Minister as to the operation of a scheme which, in the opinion of the Minister, could not be considered by a consumers' committee under the last foregoing subsection.

(3) The meetings and procedure of every committee appointed under this section shall be regulated in accordance with directions issued by the Minister for the purpose, and, for the purpose of enabling any such committee to consider any matter which it is their duty under this section to consider, the board administering the scheme to which the matter relates shall furnish the
PR

A.D. 1930.
—
Consumers'
Committees
and Com-
mittee of
Investigation.

Agricultural Marketing. [20 & 21 GEO. 5.]

committee with such accounts and other information as the committee require.

(4) If the committee of investigation reports to the Minister that any provision of a scheme or any act or omission of a board administering a scheme is contrary to the interest of consumers of the regulated product, or is contrary to the interest of any persons affected by the scheme and is not in the public interest, the Minister, if he thinks fits so to do after considering the report and consulting the Board of Trade—

(a) may by order make such amendments in the scheme as he considers necessary or expedient for the purpose of rectifying the matter;

(b) may by order revoke the scheme;

(c) in the event of the matter being one which it is within the power of the board administering the scheme to rectify, may direct that board to rectify the matter, and, if the directions are not complied with, may by order make such amendments in the scheme as he considers necessary for securing that the directions will be complied with, and in particular may by such amendments provide that the board shall, for such period as may be specified in the amendments, be composed wholly or partly of persons nominated by the Minister.

Report to
be laid
before Parliament.

8. The Minister shall, in the year nineteen hundred and thirty-two, and in each subsequent year, lay before Parliament a report upon the operation of all the schemes for the time being in force under this Act.

Agricultural Marketing Funds

A.D. 1930.
———

9. — (I) For the purpose of making loans to boards administering schemes under this Act, there shall be established and maintained a fund to be called "the Agricultural Marketing Fund" (hereinafter referred to as "the English fund"), which shall be administered and controlled by the Minister of Agriculture and Fisheries, and a fund to be called " the Agricultural Marketing (Scotland) Fund" (hereinafter referred to as "the Scottish fund"), which shall be administered and controlled by the Secretary of State for Scotland.

Agricultural Marketing Funds.

(2) *There shall be paid, out of moneys provided by Parliament into the English fund such sums, not exceeding in the aggregate five hundred thousand pounds, and into the Scottish fund such sums, not exceeding in the aggregate one hundred and twenty-five thousand pounds, as Parliament may from time to time determine.*

(3) Any such loan as aforesaid shall be made —

    (*a*) in the case of a scheme applicable both in England and in Scotland, out of both the English and the Scottish funds in such proportion as may be determined by the Minister;

    (*b*) in the case of a scheme applicable only in England, out of the English fund;

    (*c*) in the case of a scheme applicable only in Scotland, out of the Scottish fund.

(4) *Any sums received by way of interest on any such loans as aforesaid shall be paid to the Treasury, and any sums received by way of repayment of the principal of any such loan shall be paid into the fund out of which the loan was made or, in the case of a loan*

A.D. 1930.

made out of both funds, into each fund in proportion to the amount of the principal lent thereout.

(5) *If, in the opinion of the Treasury, a sum representing the whole or any part of the principal of any such loan as aforesaid is not likely to be recovered, the Treasury may direct that that sum shall be written off the account of the assets of the fund out of which the loan was made or, in the case of a loan made out of both funds, written off the account of the assets of each fund in proportion to the sum lent thereout, and there may, in addition to the sums hereinbefore mentioned, be paid into the fund out of moneys provided by Parliament an amount equal to the sum so written off, but, if any sum is received by way of repayment of the principal of a loan after it has been so written off as aforesaid, that sum shall, instead of being paid into the fund or funds out of which the loan was made, be paid to the Treasury.*

(6) The Minister shall cause an account to be prepared and transmitted to the Comptroller and Auditor General for examination on or before the thirtieth day of September in every year, showing the receipts into and issues out of the English and Scottish funds respectively in the financial year ending on the thirty-first day of March preceding, and, in a case where during that year a sum has been written off the account of the assets of the fund, giving the reasons why it appears that that sum is not likely to be recovered, and the Comptroller and Auditor General shall certify and report upon the account, and the account and report shall be laid before Parliament by the Treasury on or before the thirty-first day of January in the following year, if Parliament is then sitting, or, if Parliament is not then sitting

within one week after Parliament is next as- A.D. 1930.
sembled.

10. There shall be appointed by the Minister, Agricultural
after consultation with the Treasury, an Agricul- Marketing
tural Marketing Facilities Committee for England Committees.
and an Agricultural Marketing Facilities Committee for Scotland, and the Minister may appoint
from the members of the said committees an
Agricultural Marketing Facilities Committee for
Great Britain, and it shall be the duty of the said
committees respectively to consider, and make
recommendations with respect to, the making and
renewal of loans out of the said funds to boards
administering schemes applicable only in England,
applicable only in Scotland and applicable both
in England and in Scotland.

11.—(1) *On the approval of any scheme under* Short-term
this Act, the Minister may, on the recommendation loans.
of the appropriate Agricultural Marketing Facilities
Committee, make to the board a loan of such amount
as he thinks necessary for the purpose of providing
for expenses incurred in connection with the initial
working of the scheme.

(2) *A loan under this section shall be repaid*
within two years, unless it is renewed as hereinafter
provided, and may be made free of interest during any
period before renewal, and every such loan shall be
made on such other terms as the Minister, with the
approval of the Treasury, may by regulations
prescribe.

(3) A loan under this section shall not be renewed unless the renewal is recommended by the
appropriate Agricultural Marketing Facilities Committee, and that committee shall not recommend

Agricultural Marketing. [20 & 21 Geo. 5.]

A.D. 1930.
—

the renewal, unless they are satisfied that the board are in a position to repay the loan forthwith, that the renewal is required to provide for additional services which the board propose to undertake and that adequate arrangements have been, or will be, made to repay the loan at the expiration of the period for which it is to be renewed.

Long-term
loans.

12. *If, in the opinion of the Minister, it is expedient that there should be made to any board a loan which shall not be repayable until the expiration of a period exceeding two years, he may, on the recommendation of the appropriate Agricultural Marketing Facilities Committee, lend to that board such sums as he thinks fit, and every such loan shall be made on such terms and secured in such manner as the Minister, with the approval of the Treasury, may by regulations prescribe:*

Provided that the amount outstanding of the loans made under this section shall not at any time exceed in the aggregate one hundred thousand pounds, in the case of the English fund, or fifty thousand pounds, in the case of the Scottish fund.

Supplementary

Expenses of
Minister in
connection
with com-
mittees.

13. *Any expenses incurred by the Minister in connection with any committee appointed under this Act shall, up to an amount approved by the Treasury, be defrayed out of moneys provided by Parliament.*

Provisions
as to orders.

14.—(1) For the purpose of obtaining the approval by Parliament of the making of any order under this Act, the Minister may lay before each House of Parliament a draft of the order, and unless either House, before the expiration of the period of twenty days on which that House has sat

next after the draft is laid before it, resolves that A.D. 1930.
the order shall not be made, Parliament shall be
deemed to have approved of the making of the
order.

(2) Where Parliament have approved the
making of an order as aforesaid, the Minister may
make an order in terms of the draft to take effect
on such date after the expiration of the said period
as may be specified in the order, and the making
of the order shall be conclusive evidence that the
requirements of this Act have been complied with
and that the order, and any scheme or amendment of a scheme set out therein, has been duly
made and is within the powers conferred by this
Act.

(3) Every order made by the Minister under
this Act shall, as soon as practicable after the
making thereof, be published in the Gazette, and
every order or draft of an order approving a
scheme, or approving or making any amendment
of a scheme, shall set out the scheme or amendment, as the case may be.

15. This Act shall apply to the agricultural *Products to*
products mentioned in the Fourth Schedule to *which Act applies.*
this Act:

Provided that the Secretary of State for
Scotland and the Minister of Agriculture and
Fisheries acting in conjunction may, subject to
the approval of Parliament, by order amend the
said Schedule by adding to the products therein
mentioned any other agricultural product, and
the said Schedule shall thereupon have effect as
amended by the order.

16.—(1) In this Act, unless the context other- *Interpre-*
wise requires, the following expressions have the *tation.*
meanings hereby respectively assigned to them:—

Agricultural Marketing. [20 & 21 GEO. 5.]

"Board" means a board administering a scheme under this Act and, in relation to any scheme, means the board administering that scheme:

"Contravention" includes non-compliance, and the expression "contravene" shall be construed accordingly:

"Gazette" means—

(a) in relation to a scheme applicable only in England, the London Gazette;

(b) in relation to a scheme applicable only in Scotland, the Edinburgh Gazette;

(c) in relation to any other scheme, the London Gazette and the Edinburgh Gazette:

"Live stock" means cattle, sheep, pigs, poultry or bees:

"Minister" means—

(a) in relation to a scheme applicable both in England and in Scotland or in relation to the Agricultural Marketing Facilities Committee for Great Britain, both the Minister of Agriculture and Fisheries and the Secretary of State for Scotland acting in conjunction;

(b) in relation to a scheme applicable only in England or in relation to the English fund or in relation to the Agricultural Marketing Facilities Committee for England, the Minister of Agriculture and Fisheries;

(c) in relation to a scheme applicable only in Scotland or in relation to the Scottish fund or in relation to the Agricultural

Marketing Facilities Committee for Scotland, the Secretary of State for Scotland:

A.D. 1930.
—

"Producer" means, in relation to any scheme, any person who produces the regulated product:

"Registered producer" means, in relation to any scheme, a producer registered under the scheme:

"Regulated product" means, in relation to any scheme, any product the marketing of which is regulated by the scheme.

(2) For the purposes of a scheme regulating the marketing of live stock of any kind, every person who keeps live stock of that kind shall be deemed to produce it.

17.—This Act shall apply to Scotland subject to the following modifications:—

Application to Scotland.

(1) The following subsection shall be substituted for subsection (3) of section five:—

"(3) It shall be lawful for the board to create by instrument in writing in favour of a bank a charge on all or any of the agricultural produce in Scotland from time to time belonging to, and in the possession of, the board, as security for sums advanced or to be advanced to the board or paid or to be paid on its behalf under any guarantee by the bank, and interest, commission and charges thereon, and the provisions of Part II of the Agricultural Credits (Scotland) Act, 1929, shall apply to any charge created in pursuance of this subsection in like manner as they apply to an agricultural charge.

19 & 20 Geo. 5. c. 13.

A.D. 1930.

In this subsection the expressions 'bank' and ' agricultural produce' have the same meanings respectively as in the Agricultural Credits (Scotland) Act, 1929."

(2) For any reference in this Act to the High Court there shall be substituted a reference to the Court of Session, and for any reference therein to a county court or to the district of a county court there shall be substituted a reference to the sheriff or to the jurisdiction of the sheriff, and for paragraph (b) of the proviso to subsection (4) of section six the following paragraph shall be substituted:—

"(b) it shall be lawful for the Court of Session, on the application of the board or of any party to the contract, to require any appeal to the sheriff court under this section to be remitted to the Court of Session."

(3) If an agricultural society satisfies the Secretary of State for Scotland—

(a) that its members are substantially representative of the persons who produce an agricultural product in an area in Scotland, having regard both to the number of persons so represented and to the quantity of the product produced by them in the area; and

(b) that the society has made with each of its members who is a producer of the product in the area a contract binding him for a specified period not to sell the product produced by him otherwise than through the agency of the society;

any scheme made in pursuance of this Act for the area regulating the marketing of the product may, in lieu of constituting a board in accordance with A.D. 1930. section two of this Act, provide that the govern- ing body of the agricultural society shall be the board for the purposes of such scheme.

Provided that the Secretary of State, before approving a scheme containing any such provi- sion, shall have regard to the interests of all pro- ducers of the product in the area, whether members of the agricultural society or not.

(4) Where a scheme provides that the govern- ing body of an agricultural society shall be the board for the purposes of the scheme, the following provisions shall have effect: —

(*a*) every member of the society who is a pro- ducer of the product within the area shall be deemed to be a registered producer;

(*b*) nothing in the provisions of this Act shall render the fund referred to in section five liable for any contracts of the governing body other than contracts entered into for the purpose of the operation of the scheme, and the said fund shall not be applied directly or indirectly except for such purpose, and nothing in the said provisions shall render the funds or property of the society liable for any contracts entered into by the governing body for such purpose as aforesaid, and such funds or property shall not be ap- plied directly or indirectly for such purpose;

(*c*) nothing in the provisions of this Act with regard to the winding up of a board shall affect or apply to the society or the governing body except in its capacity as a board, or impose any liability on any member of the society except as a registered producer;

(*d*) the provisions of this Act with regard to boards (other than those relating to the composition thereof) shall apply to the governing body subject to the foregoing and to any other necessary modifications.

(5) When the governing body of an agricultural society is a board for the purposes of a scheme under this Act—

(*a*) a contract by a member of the society binding him for a specified period not to sell the regulated product produced by him otherwise than through the agency of the society shall not be held to be in restraint of trade or to be illegal on that ground; and

(*b*) it shall be lawful for a member of the society to create by instrument in writing in favour of the society a charge over any product which he is under contract to sell through the agency as security for sums advanced or to be advanced to him in anticipation of the payment of the sums received for the sale of the product.

The provisions of sections five, six, seven and eight of the Agricultural Credits (Scotland) Act, 1929, shall apply with the necessary modifications to charges created in terms of this paragraph.

(6) In this section—

"agricultural society" means a society or company registered under the Industrial and Provident Societies Acts,

1893 to 1928, or under the Companies Act, 1929, having for its object or one of its objects the sale on behalf of its members of any agricultural product, and, where any such society is so registered under the Industrial and Provident Societies Acts, 1893 to 1928, paragraph (*a*) of the proviso to section four of the Industrial and Provident Societies Act, 1893, shall in its application to such society have effect as if five hundred pounds were substituted for two hundred pounds;

"governing body," in the case of a society registered under the Industrial and Provident Societies Acts, 1893 to 1928, means the committee of management or other directing body of the society and, in the case of a company registered under the Companies Act, 1929, means the directors.

18. – (1) This Act may be cited as the Agricultural Marketing Act, 1930.

(2) This Act shall not extend to Northern Ireland.

A.D. 1930.

19 & 20
Geo. 5. c. 23.

56 & 57 Vict.
c. 39.

Short title
and extent.

A.D. 1930.

Section 1.

SCHEDULES

FIRST SCHEDULE

SUBMISSION, APPROVAL, AMENDMENT AND REVOCATION OF SCHEMES

PART I

SUBMISSION OF SCHEMES

A scheme regulating the marketing of a product to which this Act applies may be submitted by any persons who satisfy the Minister that they are substantially representative of the persons who produce that product in the area to which the scheme is applicable, and, for the purpose of satisfying himself as aforesaid, the Minister shall have regard both to the number of persons represented and to the quantity of the product produced by them in that area during some recent period before the scheme is submitted.

PART II

APPROVAL OF SCHEMES

1. Before approving a scheme the Minister shall cause to be published, in the Gazette and in such other manner as he thinks best for informing persons affected, notice of his intention to approve the scheme, of the places where copies thereof may be inspected and of the time within which, and the manner in which, representations with respect to the scheme may be made.

2. The Minister, after considering any scheme duly submitted to him and any representations

duly made with respect thereto and after holding such inquiries (if any) as he thinks fit, may, if he is satisfied that the scheme will conduce to the more efficient production and marketing of the regulated product and to the stabilisation of the price thereof, approve the scheme with or without modifications:

A.D. 1930.

Provided that —

    (a) no such modifications shall enlarge the area to which the scheme is applicable; and

    (b) before approving the scheme with modifications, the Minister shall give notice of the proposed modifications to the persons who submitted the scheme, and, if within three weeks after notice has been so given, those persons notify the Minister that they desire to withdraw the scheme, the Minister shall not approve it.

PART III

AMENDMENT AND REVOCATION OF SCHEMES

1st Sch.
—*cont.*

1. If the board administering a scheme submit to the Minister an amendment of the scheme, the Minister may by order approve the amendment, so, however, that the provisions of this Act relating to the approval of schemes shall, so far as applicable, apply in relation to the approval of any such amendment.

2. The Minister shall by order revoke a scheme regulating the marketing of any product —

    (a) if an order is made for the winding up of the board administering the scheme,

A.D. 1980.

(*b*) if a subsequent scheme regulating the marketing of that product comes into force in an area comprising the area to which the first-mentioned scheme applies.

3. The Minister may by order revoke a scheme, if the board administering the scheme satisfy him that the revocation of the scheme is desired by more than half the registered producers.

4. Without prejudice to any other powers conferred on him by this Act, the Minister, if he is of opinion that any provision of a scheme or any act or omission of a board administering a scheme is contrary to the interest of consumers of the regulated product, or is contrary to the interest of a substantial number of persons affected by the scheme and is not in the public interest, may make an order, subject to the approval of Parliament, amending or revoking the scheme.

5. The board administering a scheme shall not be deemed to be dissolved by reason only that the scheme has been revoked, and so much of the scheme as relates to the winding up of the board shall continue in force notwithstanding the revocation.

52 & 53 Vict, c. 63.

6. Where a scheme is revoked, subsection (2) of section thirty-eight of the Interpretation Act, 1889, (which relates to the effect of repeals) shall apply as if the revocation of the scheme were the repeal of an enactment by another Act.

SECOND SCHEDULE

Section 2.

Provisions as to the Incorporation, Registration and Winding up of Boards

1. The board shall be constituted by the scheme as a body corporate with a common seal

and power to hold land without licence in mort-
main.

2. The scheme shall provide for notification to the Minister of the address of the office of the board at which communications and notices will at all times be received, and of any change in that address, and the Minister shall cause a register to be kept showing the address of every board, and the register shall be open for inspection by the public at such times and at such place as he may direct.

3. The scheme shall provide for the winding up of the board, and for that purpose may apply Part X of the Companies Act, 1929, subject to the modifications hereafter set out in this Schedule.

4. For the purpose of section three hundred and thirty-eight of the Companies Act, 1929, the principal place of business of the board shall be deemed to be the office of the board registered by the Minister under this Act.

5. Sub-paragraph (ii) of paragraph (*e*) of subsection (1) of section three hundred and thirty-eight of the Companies Act 1929, shall not apply, and sub-paragraph (iii) of that paragraph shall apply as if the words "or any member thereof as such" were omitted.

6. A petition for winding up the board may be presented by the Minister as well as by any person authorised under the other provisions of the Companies Act, 1929, to present a petition for winding up a company.

7. Every person who, at any time during the relevant period, was a registered producer shall, for the purpose of subsection (1) of section three hundred and thirty-nine of the Companies Act, 1929, be liable to contribute to the payment of the debts and liabilities of the board and to the

Q R

payment of the costs and expenses of the winding up such proportion as may be provided in the scheme of the aggregate amount of the sums paid or payable to him in respect of the sale of the regulated product during that period.

8. In the last foregoing paragraph the expression "the relevant period" means—
    (*a*) in the case where, before the commencement of the winding up, the scheme has been revoked, the year immediately before the revocation of the scheme;
    (*b*) in any other case, the year immediately before the commencement of the winding up.

Section 4.

THIRD SCHEDULE

ADDITIONAL MATTERS FOR WHICH SCHEMES MUST PROVIDE

1. As to the accounts to be kept by the board and as to the audit of such accounts.

2. As to the furnishing by the board to the Minister and to registered producers of copies of accounts, returns and other information.

3. As to the furnishing by the board of a copy of the last balance sheet of the board to any person requiring it.

4. As to the estimates, returns, accounts and other information to be furnished to the board by registered producers.

5. As to the powers of persons authorised by the board to enter and inspect, at any reasonable time, any land or premises occupied by a registered producer, and to inspect and take copies of any books, accounts or other documents kept by him relating to the regulated product.

FOURTH SCHEDULE

Products to Which Act applies

A.D. 1930.
—
Section 15.

Milk.
Potatoes.
Hops.
Wool.
Cereals.
Cheese.
Live stock.

Q R*

APPENDIX V

Abuse of the Dole

" IF then the great officers of State reckon up at the end of the year how much the dole brings in, how much it adds to their income, what shall we dependants do who, out of the self-same dole, have to find ourselves in coats and shoes, in the bread and fire of our homes? A mob of litters comes in quest of the hundred farthings; here is a husband going the round, followed by a sickly or pregnant wife; another, by a clever and well-known trick, claims for a wife that is not there, pointing, in her stead, to a closed and empty chair: 'My Galla's in there,' says he; 'let us off quick, will you not?' 'Galla, put out your head!' 'Don't disturb her, she's asleep!'

Juvenal: *Satire* I.

Bread and Games

"And what does the mob of Remus say? It follows fortune, as it always does, and rails against the condemned. That same rabble, if Nortia had smiled upon the Etruscan, if the aged Emperor had been struck down unawares, would in that very hour have conferred upon Sejanus the title of Augustus. Now that no one buys our votes, the public has long since cast off its cares; the people that once bestowed commands, consulships, legions and all else, now meddles no more and longs eagerly for just two things – Bread and Games!"

Juvenal: *Satire* 10.

The Convenience of the Lazy Plebeians

"Yet the name of that city was still pronounced with respect: the frequent and capricious tumults of its inhabitants were indulged with impunity; and the successors of Constantine, instead of crushing the last remains of the democracy by the strong arm of military power, embraced the mild policy of Augustus, and studied to relieve the poverty, and to amuse the idleness, of an innumerable people. I. For the convenience of the lazy plebeians the monthly distributions of corn were converted into a daily allowance of bread; a great number of ovens was constructed and maintained at the public expense; and at the appointed hour each citizen who was furnished with a ticket ascended the flight of steps which had been assigned to his peculiar quarter or division, and received, either as a gift or at a very low price, a loaf of bread of the weight of three pounds for the use of his family."

Gibbon: *The Decline and Fall of the Roman Empire*
(Chap. xxxi., A.D. 408).

Character of the People

"Yet, as long as the people bestowed, by their suffrages, the honours of the State, the command of the legions, and the administration of wealthy provinces, their conscious pride alleviated, in some measure, the hardships of poverty; and their wants were seasonably supplied by the ambitious liberality of the candidates, who aspired to secure a venal majority in the thirty-five tribes, or the hundred and ninety-three centuries, of Rome. But, when the prodigal commons had imprudently alienated not only the *use*, but the *inheritance*, of power, they sunk, under the reign of the Cæsars, into a vile and wretched populace which must, in a few generations, have been totally extinguished, if it had not been continually recruited by the manumission of slaves and the influx of strangers. As early as the time of Hadrian it was the just complaint of the ingenuous natives that the capital had attracted the vices of the universe and the manners of the most opposite nations. The intemperance of the Gauls, the cunning and levity of the Greeks, the savage obstinacy of the Egyptians and Jews, the servile temper of the Asiatics, and the dissolute, effeminate prostitution of the Syrians, were mingled in the various multitude, which, under the proud and false denomination of Romans, presumed to despise their fellow-subjects, and even their sovereigns, who dwelt beyond the precincts of the ETERNAL CITY."

Gibbon: *The Decline and Fall of the Roman Empire*
(Chap. xxxi., A.D. 408).

" . . . et Circenses"

"But the most lively and splendid amusement of the idle multitude depended on the frequent exhibition of public games and spectacles . . . the Roman people still considered the Circus as their home, their temple, and the seat of the republic. The impatient crowd rushed at the dawn of day to secure their places, and there were many who passed a sleepless and anxious night in the adjacent porticos. From the morning to the evening, careless of the sun or of the rain, the spectators, who sometimes amounted to the number of four hundred thousand, remained in eager attention; their eyes fixed on the horses and charioteers, their minds agitated with hope and fear, for the success of the *colours* which they espoused; and the happiness of Rome appeared to hang on the event of a race."

Gibbon: *The Decline and Fall of the Roman Empire*
(Chap. xxxi., A.D. 408).

The Breakdown of Administration

"But the unscientific and inefficient financial system will chiefly attract the notice of the historical enquirer. . . . Still more fatal to pure administration was the system which left to the municipal class the assessment and collection of the revenue in their district. That doomed order are at once branded as the worst oppressors, and invested with the melancholy glory of being the martyrs of a ruinous system of finance. Their lingering fate, recorded in 192 edicts, a tragedy prolonged through more than five generations, is one of the most curious examples of obstinate and purblind legislation, contending hopelessly with inexorable laws of society and human nature. In that contest the middle or bourgeois class was almost extinguished, Roman financial administration was paralysed, and at its close the real victors were the great landholders, surrounded by their serfs and dependants. A volume might be written on the corruption and cruel oppression of the officials of the treasury, servile to the great, tyrannical to the poor, and calmly defying all the menaces of the Emperor in their unchecked career of rapacity. The last and deepest impression which the enquirer will carry with him, as he rises from a study of the Theodosian Code, is that fraud and greed are everywhere triumphant, that the rich are growing richer and more powerful, while the poor are becoming poorer and more helpless, and that the imperial government, inspired with the best intentions, has lost all control of the vast machine.

"Yet amid all the perverse errors of legislation and the hopeless corruption of the financial service, the candid reader of the Code cannot help feeling that the central authority was keenly alive to its duties, and almost overwhelmed by its responsibilities."

> Samuel Dill: *Roman Society in the Last Century of the Western Empire* (Book III., chap. i., "The Disorganisation of the Public Service").

The Heads of the Guilds become Counts

"Of all the departments of administration, probably none caused the Emperor greater anxiety than that concerned with the food-supplies of the capital. . . . An army of public servants incorporated in hereditary guilds, Navicularii, Pistores, Suarii, Pecuarii, were charged with the duty of bringing up supplies and preparing them for consumption. . . . One of the hardest tasks of the government was to prevent the members of these guilds from deserting or evading their hereditary obligations. It is well known that the tendency of the later Empire was to stereotype society, by compelling men to follow the occupation of their fathers, and preventing a free circulation among different callings and grades of life. The man who brought the grain of Africa to the public stores at Ostia, the baker who made it into loaves for distribution, the butchers who brought pigs from Samnium, Lucania, or Bruttium, the purveyors of wine and oil, the men who fed the furnaces of the public baths, were bound to their callings from one generation to another. It was the principle of rural serfdom applied to social functions. Every avenue of escape was closed. . . . The corporati, it is true, had certain privileges, exemptions, and allowances, and the heads of some of the guilds might be raised to the rank of 'Count.' But their property, like their persons, was at the mercy of the State."

> Samuel Dill: *Roman Society in the Last Century of the Western Empire* (Book III., Chap. i., "The Disorganisation of the Public Service").

"The Game of Grab"

"When one wanders through the maze of enactments dealing with fiscal oppression, malversation, and evasion, one knows not whether more to pity the weakness of the government, or to wonder at the hardened cupidity and audacity of the classes which were leagued together in plundering both the treasury and the taxpayer."

> Samuel Dill: *Roman Society in the Last Century of the Western Empire* (Book III., Chap. ii., "The Decay of the Middle Class").

Evils aggravated by Remedies

"The system of bureaucratic despotism, elaborated finally by Diocletian and Constantine, produced a tragedy in the truest sense, such as history has seldom exhibited; in which by an inexorable fate, the claims of fancied omnipotence ended in a humiliating paralysis of administration; in which, determined effort to remedy social evils only aggravated them till they became unendurable; in which the best intentions of the central power were, generation after generation, mocked and defeated alike by irresistible laws of human nature, and by hopeless perfidy and corruption in the servants of government."

> Samuel Dill: *Roman Society in the Last Century of the Western Empire* (Book III., Chap. ii., "The Decay of the Middle Class").

Force fails to cure the Empire's Ills

"The decay had definitely set in as early as the beginning
of the second century. The wars of that century demonstrated
the hopeless weakness of the Empire and awakened the
interest of the Emperors in economic problems. But, even
when they realised the danger, they were helpless to cure the
disease. Their constructive measures were puerile and brought
no relief. To save the State they resorted to the old practice
of the ancient world – the policy of force and compulsion.
Force and compulsion were applied both to the city *bourgeoisie*
and to the lower classes, and they embittered each against
the other. The result was the collapse of city-capitalism and
the acute economic crisis of the third century, which brought
about the rapid decline of business activity in general, the
resuscitation of primitive forms of economy, and the growth
of State-capitalism. These were the salient features of life
in the fourth and following centuries."

> M. Rostovtzeff: From the Preface to his *The Social and
> Economic History of the Roman Empire.*

*Three Extracts from Tenney Frank's "An Economic History
of Rome,"* Chap. xxii., Beginnings of Serfdom.

The Decline of Letters

"The student of the political history of Rome who surveys
the reigns of the five 'good' emperors will probably gain the
impression that conditions under them were satisfactory.
If, however, he penetrates deeply into the cultural history
of the time he learns that this impression is incorrect. Roman
literature, for instance, came to an end with Tacitus and
Juvenal. There is not one Latin poem or essay of even fifth-
rate quality in the century that follows, not one penetrating
work of criticism or philosophy, not one good original narra-
tive in prose or verse. There is not even any learned work of
value. Mental vitality and the creative faculty seem to have
disappeared. This is a fact of first-rate significance, for we
cannot point to any period of history where such mental torpor

continued through a long period of sound social and economic conditions."

The Breakdown of Municipal Government

"In political administration, self-government was failing everywhere. Trajan had to send out personal representatives to the provinces to check the accounts, to correct abuses, and to give advice to the local governments, while Hadrian extended the system of 'correctors' to the cities of Italy itself. In jurisprudence there still seems to have been some vitality left, for the task of adapting and interpreting the old legal principles to an ever-growing citizenry in the provinces called for able minds. But it is noteworthy that the very jurists who attempted this task were the ones who began to lay the basis in the Roman code for imperial despotism. Evidently they no longer had any faith in the capacity of the people to think soundly or govern wisely."

A Façade of Prosperity

"Rome still seemed prosperous to the casual observer, but it was a thin prosperity lasting on through peaceful times without creating surplus resources for future contingencies."